For years I've encouraged communicators to answer two simple questions before standing up to speak: What do you want your audience to know, and what do you want them to do? In Communicating for a Change, *Andy Stanley provides us with a communication strategy built around these two fundamental questions. Whether you are a senior pastor with weekly teaching responsibilities or a student pastor who has been charged with engaging the hearts and minds of high school students, this book is a must-read."*

BILL HYBELS
Senior pastor, Willow Creek Community Church

As one of the most effective communicators in the church today, few leaders are better qualified to teach on the ins and outs of preaching than my good friend Andy Stanley. A very practical resource for every biblical communicator who wants to go from good to great."

ED YOUNG
Senior pastor, Fellowship Church, Grapevine, Texas

To communicate effectively, you have to connect. Andy has been connecting with people for years and now he's sharing his insights with the rest of us. In Communicating for a Change *you will discover how to leverage your connection as a communicator to teach people the truth of God's love, to make it have personal meaning, and to show how to live the life for which we were created."*

JEFF FOXWORTHY
Comedian

COMMUNICATING
FOR A CHANGE

ANDY STANLEY
AND LANE JONES

Multnomah Books

COMMUNICATING FOR A CHANGE
published by Multnomah Books

© 2006 by Andy Stanley and Ronald Lane Jones
International Standard Book Number: 978-1-59052-514-2

Cover image of truck by Stephen Gardner, PixelWorksStudio.net

Unless otherwise indicated, Scripture quotations are from:
The Holy Bible, New International Version
© 1973, 1984 by International Bible Society,
used by permission of Zondervan Publishing House

Published in the United States by WaterBrook Multnomah, an imprint of
The Crown Publishing Group, a division of Random House Inc., New York.

MULTNOMAH and its mountain colophon are registered trademarks
of Random House Inc.

Printed in the United States of America

For information:
MULTNOMAH BOOKS
12265 ORACLE BOULEVARD, SUITE 200
COLORADO SPRINGS, CO 80921

Library of Congress Cataloging-in-Publication Data
Stanely, Andy.
    Communicating for a change/Andy Stanely and Lane Jones
      p. cm.
    ISBN 1-59052-514-0
    1. Communication--Religious aspects--Christianity. 2. Preaching. I.
Jones, Lane. II. Title.
    BV4597.53.C64S74 2006
    251--dc22

2006013987

12—10

This book is dedicated to our friend and
partner in ministry Julie Arnold.
When it comes to creating captivating environments
and setting up communicators for success, Julie is the best.

CONTENTS

Part I
How's My Preaching?

Part II

Communicating for a Change

Acknowledgments

Most Christians can remember who was speaking the first time they heard the Scriptures taught in a way that captured their attention and created a hunger for more. For Lane and me, it was the same person. My dad. This book would not be possible apart from his influence. We would also like to thank our wives, Traci and Sandra. Specifically, we are grateful for their words of encouragement following messages where it might have been difficult to find anything encouraging to say. As always, we are grateful to Multnomah Publishers for their partnership and commitment to the local church. To our editors, Brian Thomasson and David Webb, thanks for your insight and patience.

INTRODUCTION

by Andy Stanley

I never felt called to preach. I just volunteered. I wanted to feel called. But it just never happened for me. Several of my friends felt called while we were in high school. They went forward during a Sunday night service and shared it with the congregation. Everybody clapped. Some of them are still in ministry. I think one of 'em is in jail.

One afternoon I was driving somewhere with my dad. After one of those long moments of silence that fathers and sons have when driving together, I spoke up and said, "Dad, does a person have to be called into ministry or can they just volunteer?"

He thought for a moment. "Well, I guess it's okay to volunteer."

"Good," I said. "I would like to volunteer." So I did. In fact, it was two volunteer environments that shaped me as a communicator.

During my sophomore year of college our youth pastor, Sid Hopkins, asked me if I would help him lead our Wednesday night student Bible study. That was a really strange request since we didn't even have a Wednesday night Bible study. Upon further investigation I discovered that he wanted me to *start* a study for our students. I had never led or taught anything in my life. I was a whopping two years older than some of the students I would be teaching. But I agreed to give it a try.

The good thing about being so young was that I knew what wouldn't work. Preaching wouldn't work. Teaching for twenty or thirty minutes wouldn't work. A verse by verse Bible study wouldn't work. Telling a bunch of stories and tacking on a point wouldn't work. So I decided to err on the side of simplicity. Nobody told me how long our "Bible study" was supposed to last, so I didn't feel compelled to fill up a lot of time. I had been given a blank page.

On week one about twenty students showed up. I passed out three by five cards with one verse printed on one side and a question printed on the other side. The verse for that first week was John 17:4.

"I GLORIFIED YOU ON THE EARTH, HAVING ACCOMPLISHED THE WORK WHICH YOU HAVE GIVEN ME TO DO" (NASB).

We talked about what it meant to glorify something. I explained that glorifying the Father was Christ's chief purpose for coming and that it should be ours as well. Then I had them turn the card over and spend thirty seconds thinking about an answer to the following question: What can I do this week to glorify God in my world?

Then I closed in prayer. The whole thing took about fifteen minutes. One point. One question. One application. Everybody stayed awake. Everybody was engaged. Everybody could remember what the lesson was about. Sid was a bit concerned about the brevity. But the next week the crowd grew. And it kept growing. Every week I handed out a card with a verse and a question. No music. No pizza. We didn't even have a PA system. That was my first experience as a communicator. It taught me a valuable lesson that would be reiterated a few years later.

In 1981 I moved to Dallas, Texas to attend Dallas Theological Seminary. At the end of my first semester, the principal of a local Christian high school asked me if I would present a message for their weekly chapel service. I accepted. Since it was high school students I decided I should pick a narrative portion of Scripture. Somehow I landed on the story of Naaman and Elisha. Naaman was the captain of the army of Aram. Elisha was…well, you know who Elisha was. Anyway, Naaman has leprosy and Elisha sends him to take a dip in the river. Naaman obeys and is healed.

I spent hours pouring over the story. I drew upon my vast knowledge as a first semester seminarian. I went to the library and researched the Arameans. I had pages of notes. I had an outline that went something like this: Naaman's Problem, Naaman's Pride, Namaan's Plea, Namaan's Proof. I was so overprepared.

The night before I was to give the message I was down beside my bed praying. I started praying for the students I was going to speak to the next day. I didn't know any of them personally, But I knew that from their perspective this was going to be just another chapel led by yet another unknown chapel speaker. Yawn. As I was praying, it occurred to me that they weren't going to remember one thing I said five minutes after I said it. I had spent hours preparing a lesson that no one was going to remember! What a waste of time and energy.

I got up off my knees, sat back down at my desk and determined not to let that happen. I got rid of my alliterated points and boiled it down to one idea. Then I worked on it until I had crafted a statement upon which I could hang the entire message.

The next day I told the story. I concluded with the idea that sometimes God will ask us to do things we don't understand. And that the only way to fully understand is to obey. We will all look back with a sigh of relief or feel the pain of regret. Then I delivered my statement: To understand why, submit and apply. I repeated it several times. I had them repeat it. Then I closed.

When I left the platform that day I knew I had connected. What I didn't realize at the time was that I had stumbled onto something that would shape my approach to communication.

Two years later, on a Sunday morning, a college student walked up to me and said, "Hey, you're that guy. You spoke at my high school chapel." Then he paused, collected his thoughts and said, "To understand why, submit and apply." He smiled, "I still remember," he said. Then he turned and walked away. He didn't remember my name. I never knew his. None of that mattered. What mattered was that those thirty minutes in chapel two years earlier were not a waste of time after all. One simple, well-crafted truth had found its mark in the heart of a high school student.

That Sunday morning was a defining moment. Since then I have prepared hundreds of outlines and preached hundreds of sermons. But my goal has been the same since that exasperating night in my efficiency apartment wrestling with the story of Namaan. Every time I stand to communicate I want to take one simple truth and lodge it in the heart of the listener. I want them to know that one thing and know what to do with it.

For the next couple hundred pages I'm going to download everything I have learned these past twenty years about developing an entire talk around one point. And I hope that at the end of our time together you will be willing to try some new things. Take some risks. Move out of your comfort zone as a communicator.

To help make our time together more enjoyable, my good friend and ministry partner Lane Jones has written a fascinating parable about a pastor who knew he needed to upgrade his communication skills but didn't know where to turn for help. Nobody understands my communication style better than Lane. He has trained hundreds of pastors and teachers in the method contained in this book. He gets the credit for forcing me to sit down and begin a dialogue about my approach to preaching and teaching.

The material is outlined around seven "imperatives." We chose these seven because we believe they are most critical to the process of engaging and inspiring an audience with one solitary idea. Every sermon should take the audience somewhere. We are convinced that these seven things are critical to the journey.

Throughout the book we will use the terms "sermons," "talks," "teachings," and "messages" interchangeably. Also, we make no distinction between preaching, teaching, or general communicating. For our purposes they are all the same. These seven imperatives apply in some form to all three disciplines.

As you read along you may find yourself wondering, *Isn't this just the way Andy communicates? Don't I need my own style? Surely this isn't for everybody.* Chapter sixteen addresses that issue specifically and in detail.

One last thing. You will discover quickly that I am not a fan of fill in the blank outlines in a Sunday morning environment. However, when I communicate in a seminar or leadership training environment, I almost always use handouts with blanks to be filled in. Some have wondered if I'm teaching one thing while modeling something different. Not so.

As you are about to discover in chapter one, a communicator's approach to communicating must support their goal. My goal on Sunday morning is very different than my goal in most training environments. So I've adjusted my approach. In a seminar environment the goal is usually not life change. The goal in those environments is information transfer. An outline allows a communicator to cover more material in less time. In a preaching environment, less is more.

I hope you enjoy the book. If nothing else it is a glimpse into my world; a world where every day seems to be Sunday and I am expected to have something significant to say. The expectations are unrealistic. The pressure never goes away. But I can't imagine doing anything else with my life. And the fact that you have chosen to read a book on this topic tells me that you feel the same way.

Part

1

HOW'S MY

PREACHING?

1

NO ONE'S LISTENING

He'd seen them all before. Sometimes even in his sleep.

The blank stares and faraway looks that told him he wasn't connecting. Again.

Even as he continued to preach his message, another part of Pastor Ray Martin's brain rehearsed a series of familiar observations.

There's John Phillips, sitting there trying to decide which stocks to dump tomorrow morning when the market opens. And there's his wife beside him, trying to decide whether or not to dump him. And Sally Kennedy, in her normal spot two rows from the back... A great location to keep tabs on who's here and who's not. And Norma Reed next to her, ready to supply the reason for anyone being missing.

They were all parked before him, listening to the message—or at least pretending to listen—as he tried his best to make the Word of God come alive in the twenty-first century.

Their distraction began to distract Ray. He found himself wondering if this was why those old fundamentalist preachers used to yell and pound the pulpit. It was no easy matter to keep a congregation's attention.

He felt a sudden, wild impulse to simply pick up his notes and walk off the platform. Had anyone ever done that? Just stopped preaching and walked out the back door? Would anyone even notice?

Just stare at the back wall, he told himself. It was an old trick he'd learned from a seminary professor. Just get through it; you'll be back next week. Hopefully they will, too.

Driving home that afternoon, he rehearsed the comments of the congregation that morning as he shook hands at the door after the service.

"Nice job, pastor."

"What a blessing, pastor."

"One of your best, pastor."

That last one was particularly cruel, since the comparison wasn't qualified. Like telling your wife that, for her, her hair looked pretty good that day.

He wanted to ask them all if they had learned anything. But, ultimately, he wasn't sure if that was a fair question. If *he* couldn't answer it, why should they be able to?

"It shouldn't be this hard," Ray said to no one as he turned in to his driveway.

His wife, Sally, met him at the door for their Sunday afternoon ritual. They'd done this for the ten years that Ray had been pastor of Meadowland Community Church. Ray often looked forward to the message postmortem...but not lately.

"So how do you feel it went?" she asked, giving away her opinion.

"I don't know," he lied. "How do you feel it went?"

"Fine."

When all your wife and number one cheerleader can muster is a "fine," then you know it's worse than you think. Ray sank down into the sofa. "I just don't know, sweetheart. I don't know what I'm doing anymore. I hate to say this, but Sunday morning has become just thirty minutes to fill. Thirty minutes that I start dreading an hour after I've finished the last sermon."

"That's a lot of dread, Ray. It can't be that bad. Your messages are fine—and you do a good job delivering them."

"Honey, if you worked all week to prepare a meal for me, and I said it was fine and that you did a good job delivering it, just how long would I be sleeping on the couch?"

"Oh—you know what I mean," she said.

Ray did know what she meant. She meant that it was fine, but fine wasn't good enough anymore.

"There has to be a simple solution to this," he finally said to Sally. "I must be overthinking it. Either that or it's something I've never heard before."

"Why don't you call that baseball guy?" Sally asked.

"What baseball guy?"

"The rich guy that got you so excited about trying new ideas at the church."

Pete Harlan. It had been almost six months since Ray had spent a memorable evening at the local major league ballpark, watching a game from the owner's seats. Things had gotten pretty complicated at the church, and a friend arranged for Ray to meet with Pete. A very successful businessman, Pete had shared with Ray seven practices that he had used to build his business empire. Seven practices that Ray and his elder board had been implementing with some encouraging success.

"What would Pete know about preaching?"

"That's what I asked you about church ministry, but you came home and changed everything. I figured if he could do that for the organizational side of things, maybe he can snap you out of this, too."

"I don't need to be snapped out of anything—and I really don't think Pete can help!"

"Well," she replied quietly, "then you really don't have anything to lose, do you?"

"I don't even know where his number is." Ray was in no mood to call anyone.

"Do you mean the number that's stuck in the corner of the framed picture of you throwing the ceremonial first pitch that night? The picture sitting on the mantle with Pete's card sticking out so everyone who comes into our house can see it? Is that the number you're talking about?" Sally was in no mood for a husband in a mood.

There were times when Ray wondered why he loved her so much. But this wasn't one of them. He knew he needed some advice and that Pete was indeed a wise man.

"Well, he did say to call if there was anything he could do," Ray said. "I'll call him tomorrow." It had been an hour since church had ended and Ray knew the dread was coming.

Traffic was light for a Monday as Ray drove toward La Frontera, a local Mexican restaurant he and Sally often frequented. It had good food at a cheap price, and the low prices made it an interesting choice for Pete Harlan.

Ray smiled in spite of himself. One of the richest guys in town, Pete picked one of Ray's regular spots to meet him for lunch. *I guess there's a reason he has so much money—and hangs onto it,* Ray said to himself.

He pulled into a parking space next to a gleaming white Mercedes with a vanity plate that said "Pete." Apparently, car purchases weren't one of the areas where Pete felt inclined to economize.

Pete Harlan sat in a booth, smiling at Ray's approach. Ray remembered the first time he'd seen Pete. A short, middle-aged man whose demeanor belied his position in the community, Pete could've been any one of a dozen guys already digging into the chips and salsa.

"Ray! It's great to see you again," Pete said with genuine excitement.

"Thanks so much for seeing me on such short notice."

"No problem. Things pretty much run themselves these days, and that frees up a lot of my time."

"An organization that runs itself...now that would be nice." Even as the words left his mouth, Ray knew instinctively what Pete's response would be.

"Well, Ray, if you work hard enough at those seven practices I gave you, then by the time you're my age you should have plenty of time on your hands, too."

Ray then spent the better part of an hour—and a Burrito Grande—updating Pete on life at Meadowland and the changes he'd been making. He also unloaded the reason for their meeting that day. He talked of the frustration of working as hard as he could at something, only to see himself fail again and again.

"I wouldn't call you a failure, Ray," Pete finally said. "Your sermons aren't as bad as others I've heard."

A wry smile crossed the pastor's face. "Now that's some consolation right there. I'm not the worse communicator that Pete Harlan has ever... Wait a minute, when did you ever hear me preach?"

"Oh, I've got my sources," Pete said with a grin. "I keep in touch with Joe, and I asked him to give me a couple of your tapes." Joe Dickinson was the mutual friend who had introduced Pete to Ray. "I told Joe that I had to keep an eye on my investment."

Pete *had* invested in Ray that night, sharing a lifetime of wisdom in a few short hours. *A few million in the building fund would be nice, too*, Ray thought.

"Those message tapes are a great idea. If they'd had those when I was younger, I might've gotten into church a little more—or maybe a little more church might have gotten into me. You can listen in the car if you find yourself with some drive time—and make the time count. And I like the fact that you can rewind if you don't get something. That doesn't work with a live preacher!"

Pete sipped on his iced tea then looked up into Ray's eyes. "How do *you* feel when you listen to them?"

"Listen to them? I don't even want to see them—much less listen to them."

"Practice number seven," Pete said in a matter of fact tone.

Practice number seven. Ray knew it well and it embarrassed him to have been caught red-handed. "*Work On It*. Practice number seven is to work on my ministry, not just in it. I know Pete, but this is different. This is...painful."

"Imagine how your congregation feels," he said with a twinkle in his eye.

"Thanks a lot."

"Seriously, Ray, how in the world do you expect to get any better if you don't listen to yourself? You can't fix it if you don't know where it's broken. Step one is, you've got to start listening to yourself."

"Okay, you're right. Step one: Start listening to myself, no matter how painful. What's step number two?"

"I have no idea," Pete said and then sat quietly.

After a moment, Ray broke the silence. "What do you mean you have no idea? You're the answer man. Don't you have nine practices for perfect preaching?"

"Nope. But that was nice alliteration. Maybe you should try some of that, it might help."

Pete could tell that Ray was getting frustrated. "What were you expecting, Ray? I'm a businessman, not a preacher. Did you think I was going to wave a magic wand and turn you into Willy Graham?"

"Billy."

"What?"

"His name is Billy Graham. You called him Willy."

"I know who Billy Graham is, and I meant Willy Graham. Billy Graham is good, but he's no Willy Graham."

By this time Ray was either angry or confused—he really wasn't sure. "Who's Willy Graham?"

"Willy is the best communicator I've ever known. There's not a finer man alive, as far as I'm concerned."

"And this Willy Graham is a better preacher than Billy Graham?"

"Well, Willy would never say that. That's *my* opinion. Willy used to speak all over the country, and there were many times that I made sure I was wherever he was. In fact, I knew a lot of men who would rearrange their schedules if they knew Willy was coming."

Ray wasn't convinced. "So what makes this guy so special?"

"Hard to say. I just know that whenever he finished it was like he was talking to me, personally. And I always walked away with something that would help me. I didn't always do what he said, but that was my problem, not Willy's."

"Well, I'd sure like to know his secret." Ray couldn't keep the bitter edge out of his voice. "I don't know when I last helped someone. In my business, there's not much you won't do for that kind of impact."

"Well, I'm glad to hear that, Ray."

"Why?" Ray was suspicious now. He didn't like the look in Pete's eyes.

"Willy's agreed to meet with you, and you leave right after lunch."

"*What?*" Ray had to process this. "Well, okay. I guess that works. Where do I meet him? Is he coming here?"

Pete raised one eyebrow. "Not exactly."

"Pete, I don't know you well, but I don't think I like that look. Just where do I meet Willy?"

"Atlanta."

"Atlanta? That's in Georgia, Pete."

"So they tell me."

"That's like…a thousand miles away."

"Well, you'd better get started then," Pete said as he paid the check. "Sally, that's your wife's name right?"

Ray nodded.

"I called Sally this morning and she packed you a bag. I told Joe to let the church know you'd be gone a little while. He said the elder board would be a little curious, but that he would handle them and not to worry. In the long run, they'll be glad you took the time."

Ray's head was spinning. Sally and Joe were involved in this plot? The elders were asking questions and now he was supposed to up and leave? This had to be stopped. "Wait a minute, Pete. Taking me to lunch is one thing, but this is a little much."

"Really? I thought you just said there was nothing you wouldn't do for that kind of impact."

"I know, Pete, but Atlanta is a fourteen-hour drive and I've got things to do at the office. Not to mention that I've got to get ready to preach this Sunday..."

"Which brings us back to why you called me, Ray. Now what was it you wanted help with?"

"I know, but..." Ray began to object, but Pete would have none of it.

"No buts. You called for my help, and this is my help. Take it or leave it."

It was easy to see how Pete Harlan had built his fortune.

Ray sat there not knowing what to do. It seemed like a wild goose chase. Traveling halfway across the country to meet some guy named Willy Graham. Ridiculous! Billy Graham would be one thing, but Willy? What Ray said next was more an indication of his desperation than his common sense.

"Where in Atlanta, Pete?"

"You let me worry about that. You just drive to this address, and I'll take it from there."

Ray followed the directions Pete had given him and ended up at Harlan Enterprises.

"Are you Ray?" a woman asked as Ray walked through the door. "We've been expecting you for half an hour."

"Traffic…," Ray said slowly.

"Don't worry. We can get you there in plenty of time. Just go down this corridor, down the steps, and out the door. The helicopter is on the pad."

"Helicopter?"

2

WHERE THERE'S A WILL THERE'S A RAY

A limousine was waiting just outside the Peachtree Dekalb Airport on the north side of Atlanta. The helicopter ride had been Ray's first, as was the trip in Pete's corporate jet—a sleek Gulfstream IV. For that matter, it was Ray's first ride in any kind of private plane. Now he understood why it was the toy to end all toys for the rich and famous. Three and a half hours after walking out of the Mexican restaurant, Ray was riding in style through the winding streets of Peachtree Corners, a middle-class suburb of Atlanta.

Soaking in the quiet luxury of the limo, Ray searched his memory for any recollection of Willy Graham. Now that was a name you'd remember. Ray wasn't what you would call "connected," but he was aware of most well-known preachers. Atlanta was known for a few large and successful churches, but Willy—William, maybe?—Graham's name still didn't ring a bell. After a short ride, the limo pulled into a nice subdivision of midsize homes with well-kept yards. Judging by the size of the Bradford pear trees, Ray guessed the homes were about fifteen years old. The car slowed and turned into the driveway of an attractive two-story brick home. A man stood on the front steps.

"You must be Ray," the man said as he extended his hand. "I'm Will Graham."

"I thought it was Willy," Ray offered as he shook his hand.

Will laughed. "That Pete is something, isn't he? He gets a kick out of calling me Willy Graham because Billy Graham is probably the only preacher he knows by name. You can call me Will. So what brings you to Atlanta?"

Ray wasn't sure if this was a legitimate question or not. Surely Pete had told this man why he was sending a thirty-five-year old stranger to his home. "Well, Pete thought you could help me out, I guess."

"But you're not so sure."

Ray was silent.

"That's okay, Ray. I'd be worried about you if you weren't worried about me."

Will was an affable man with an easygoing air. There was no apparent reason for Ray to be anxious.

"Is there some reason I should worry, Will?"

"Not really. It's just that I wouldn't blame a guy in your position for having his doubts about a man from my background," Will answered.

"Speaking of which," Ray began, "I've been trying to place you, but I don't think I'm familiar with your church."

"With my what?"

"Pete didn't tell me what church you're with, or were with, if you're retired now," Ray continued.

"Exactly what *did* Pete tell you about me?"

"That you are the best preacher he's ever heard, that you've spoken all over the country, and that if anyone can help me to be a better communicator, it's you. Is there more?"

Will let out a laugh that made Ray want to smile and tremble at the same time. "Ray, I'm afraid you've been brought here under somewhat false pretenses."

"Aren't you Willy Graham and aren't you a preacher?"

"Well, I am Will Graham, but I'm not a preacher by trade. For thirty-eight years I drove eighteen-wheel tankers for Harlan Petroleum."

"You're a truck driver?" Ray was feeling a little weak. "But Pete said people would come from all over to hear you preach."

"Well, that part is true. Most of what I know about preaching—or life for that matter—came from driving a truck. Every Sunday, wherever I was on the road, I'd hold service in a local truck stop or restaurant. I developed quite a following. Pete would stop by any time he was in the area. I don't think he applied very much of what he heard, but I can assure you he heard the truth."

Ray was speechless. He had flown over a thousand miles to learn to preach from a *truck driver?*

"I'm not sure what to say," he finally mumbled. "I guess that explains why you've spoken all over the country."

"Well, I can see that you're disappointed, Ray," Will began. "Pete obviously thought you could benefit from spending some time with me, but if you're having second thoughts…"

"It's not that… Well okay, it *is* that. It's just that…you're a truck driver, for crying out loud!" Ray's frustration finally spilled out.

"I don't blame you for being upset. But you're here now and Pete's plane won't be back to get you before tomorrow. Why don't we make the best of it? "

"Make the best of it?" Ray asked sarcastically. "You mean this isn't the best? I flew halfway across the country to learn communication from a truck driver and you're telling me it can get better than this?"

"Why *are* you here, Ray? Why *did* you fly halfway across the country? It wasn't because of who I am, or who I'm not for that matter. You need to ask yourself why." With that the old man walked around the corner of his house and disappeared from sight.

3

GO FOR THE GOAL

Ray waited for a few minutes for Will to reappear. Soon it became apparent that he wasn't coming back. Ray felt strange as he crept around the corner of the house into the backyard. Front yards are accessible. They are the foyers of the outside world. But a backyard is different. Ray felt as if he were snooping around in Will's house; opening drawers and closet doors. *But he left me no choice*, Ray thought. Ray tried to look through the rear windows for any sign of Will. Now he really was snooping. *What else am I supposed to do? I'm a stranger in town and have no idea where I am.*

"Are you looking for me?" Will's voice startled Ray and he turned around quickly. Will was sitting in an old Adirondack chair under the canopy of a giant oak tree.

"I wasn't sure if you were coming back," Ray stammered.

"Coming back? I never went anywhere."

Ray couldn't tell if he had offended Will by his reaction earlier. Not that he would've blamed Will. Ray sat down in the chair across from Will and dropped his overnight bag on the ground. The yard was cool and quiet. "So, what do we do now?" Ray finally broke the silence.

"That's entirely up to you, Ray, but I'd still like you to answer my question."

"What question, Will?"

"Why are you here?"

Ray thought for a moment. A thousand things went through his mind. He wanted to be a better communicator. He wanted to be excited about preaching again. He was there for many reasons but none of them seemed like the answer to the question Will was asking.

"Let me put it another way," Will said. "You may be asking yourself, 'If this guy is such a great communicator then why wasn't he a preacher instead of an over–the–road hauler? And that would be a fair question."

"And?" Ray asked.

"And I'd say it was never my goal to be a preacher. My goal was to see the country and meet as many interesting people as I could and tell them about my relationship with Jesus Christ. You see, Ray, my goal didn't lead me to be a pastor, it lead me to be a trucker."

"Why not an evangelist?" Ray asked.

"Funny thing, Ray, I always thought I was an evangelist."

"Right. Sorry about that. But, Will, I don't see what this has to do with my preaching."

"Ray, my goal to see places and meet new people determined what I did for a living. And that led to the first imperative of communication that I learned from being a trucker.

"Imperative?"

"I know it sounds kind of strong, Ray, but on the open road there's no room for indecisiveness. Just look at signs along the road; Stop... Do Not Enter... Wrong Way! All imperatives because when your life's on the line there's no time for discussion."

"Fortunately no one's life is on the line when I preach," Ray laughed.

"No, just where they spend eternity." Will wasn't laughing.

"Right. So what is the first imperative?"

"Well, like I said it was my goal to see the world that led me to be a trucker and so, before you start to communicate: *Determine Your Goal*."

Will could tell that Ray was still not with him. "Before we talk about *how* to communicate, we need to talk about *why* to communicate. What is your goal as a communicator?"

"Um…I guess to make sure that people understand the Bible."

"So your goal is understanding."

"Well…understanding is important isn't it?"

"Sure it is…but is it the most important thing?"

"What do you mean?"

"Ray, I'm going to tell you everything I know about how to effectively communicate. But if you have the wrong goal, I'll only help you get better at doing the wrong thing."

"Will, I'm lost."

"Well, son, the first thing we need to do is get you saved, then we'll work on your preaching." Now it was Ray's turn not to laugh. "Ray, have you ever heard the question, 'Are you teaching the Bible to people or…'"

"Are you teaching people the Bible," Ray finished the thought. "Yeah, I heard that in seminary."

"And what does that mean to you?"

"It means that we shouldn't be so focused on teaching the Bible that we forget that our real goal is to teach people."

"So there it is."

"There's what?"

"Your goal. You used the word goal. You said your real goal is to teach people the Bible."

"Yeah, I guess I did, didn't I. My goal is to teach people the Bible," Ray said with an air of satisfaction.

"You see what I mean, Ray, it's good to have a clear goal. Even if it is the wrong one."

Ray was caught off guard. "What? That's the wrong goal? I thought you said that teaching people was the goal?"

"Actually, Ray, you said it. I only repeated it."

"So are you saying that teaching the Bible *to* people is the goal?"

"Well, it certainly is a goal, I guess, but I wouldn't call it *the* goal."

Ray was getting a little tense. "Then what is *the* goal?"

"Now that is the question, isn't it?" Will said as he stood and stretched. "Look, Ray, it's not important that you know what the goal is right now. It's enough that you know what it's not."

"Why is that enough?"

"Because now you're ready to adapt your approach to communication."

"Adapt it to what?"

"The real goal. Is that your only bag?"

Ray nudged the small overnight bag with his foot. "Yeah, my wife packed for me and I'd have to say it's a little light. Where do you want me to put it?"

"Wait right here."

Will disappeared into the garage. In a moment he reappeared, this time in the cab of one of the biggest pickup trucks Ray had ever seen. "Throw it in the back and climb in."

By this time Ray had become accustomed to following orders. He obediently tossed the bag in the back of the truck and climbed into the passenger seat of the massive cab. "Are you going to tell me the real goal or not, Will?"

"You'll figure it out, Ray. In fact, you already know it, you just don't know you know it."

"Well, if you're not going to tell me the goal then what are we going to do?"

"We'll talk about how to communicate for a while and the why will become clear."

"Thanks, Yoda, or do you prefer Obi Wan?"

The look on Will's face made it clear to Ray that Will had missed the Star Wars generation.

"Well," Will began, "as I said, most of what I know about preaching came from driving a truck. I don't drive the big rigs anymore. This here is the biggest thing I tackle these days." Will patted the massive dashboard as if it were a pet.

Ray couldn't help but think that size was relative. Will didn't drive the big rigs anymore, but what he did drive seemed twice the size of Ray's minivan. Will pulled out onto the street and drove a few minutes in silence as Ray studied the interior of the four-door pickup. He was looking at the various gauges and indicator lights when he realized that they were merging onto an interstate highway.

"Will?"

"Yes?"

"Where are we going?"

4

THE END OF
THE ROAD

"What's that, Ray?"

"I asked where we were going."

"Why?"

"I don't know. I guess I'd just feel better if I knew where we were headed."

Will smiled and glanced at Ray in a knowing way. "And that's lesson number two, amigo. The second imperative of communication I learned from driving a truck. Before you head out on the open road: *Pick a Point.*"

The oversized pickup was actually very comfortable. The ride was smooth, the seats soft and roomy. "If the people at Meadowland could sit in a seat like this every Sunday, they wouldn't care what point we were headed to," Ray said.

"Yeah, but they'd probably go to sleep."

"That's pretty cold coming from another preacher. Even if he is a truck driver," Ray said with a smile. "So…what exactly do you mean by picking a point?"

"Just this. I've always thought of a sermon, or any talk for that matter, as a journey. You start somewhere, you go somewhere, and ultimately you end up somewhere. The question is, did you end up where you wanted to go? Now you can drive around willy-nilly and *hope* you end up somewhere interesting, or you can decide before you get behind the wheel—or the pulpit—where you're going. I'm talking about taking your audience on a journey. Taking them to a place where they discover a truth that will change their lives."

Glancing over at his passenger, Will continued. "As a driver I can get in my rig and head out across the country. And eventually, I'll get somewhere. I may even see a lot of interesting things along the way. But if I don't have a destination in mind, then I'm just out driving, aren't I?"

Ray nodded.

"You see, Ray, my effectiveness comes from knowing where I'm going and *getting there*. Preaching's the same way. I can talk about a lot of interesting stuff—and it can all be true, for that matter. But if there's no point, no ultimate destination, then all I've been doing is talking.

"You see, in my business a clear destination is vital. If you leave Atlanta to make a delivery to 'somewhere on the West Coast,' you can easily end up a thousand miles off course. Were you headed to Seattle or San Diego? See what I mean? But even knowing it's San Diego doesn't help that much when you consider the size of that city. But knowing that I'm headed for the Chevron station at 1221 Eleventh Avenue near Broadway in San Diego means that I know where I'm going before I leave."

Ray stared at Will, afraid to entertain the thoughts that were creeping into his mind. *I've traveled a thousand miles to learn to preach from Mr. Google Earth. Just how desperate am I?* Desperate enough. "So what's your point?"

"Just this. When you step up to speak, can you tell me the address you're taking me to? Can you, in a few short words—like 1221

Eleventh Avenue—eliminate all the other possible places my mind can wander over the next thirty minutes? When I get to where you want to take me, will I know I've been there? It's what I call a *one point message*, Ray."

"One point?"

"That's right. It's just like an address. It's a short, simple statement that summarizes the entire message."

"But…," Ray wasn't really sure what to say. Of course he agreed with Will that you had to have some important things to say, but *things*. Not one thing. "But I always have *plenty* to say, Will, that's not the problem. I look at a passage of Scripture and it's like it comes alive. I don't need help coming up with truth; I need to know how to make people listen."

"I'm getting the same feeling right now," Will said. "Ray, you're not listening to me. Let's try something. Ready? Forty-two, seventeen, eleven, thirty-nine, seventy-six, twenty-four, nine, twelve, eighty-four. Now, repeat those numbers back to me."

"Well…I can't do that. I can't remember all that."

"Good. If you could, I was going to drop you off at the next exit. Now let's try again. Forty-four, forty-four, forty-four, forty-four, FORTY-FOUR. Now repeat back the *number*."

Ray answered, but he didn't want to. "Forty-four."

"Very good. Look, I know it's a silly illustration. But it's an important point. If you give people too much to remember, they won't remember anything. They'll have forgotten all your points before they're out of the church parking lot. Everything you say can be interesting. Heck, everything you say can be life-changing; but if they can't remember it then it won't change a thing. It's like somebody said one time, 'If you're thirsty, don't go to a fire hydrant. You'll drown yourself before you ever manage a swallow.' You've got to narrow the focus of your message to one point. Then everything else in the message supports, illustrates, and helps to make it memorable."

"But I think that's what I do," Ray said defensively.

"Open that glove box." Ray complied and what he saw surprised him. Stacked neatly were about ten plastic cassette cases with tapes of sermons. Ray's sermons.

"Where did…? How did…? You couldn't have known I was…"

"Relax, man. Pete's been sendin' me those for the past six months. We send each other things, compare notes on hobbies, interests, things like that. Anyway, Pete started sending me your tapes after you guys met. He said something about protecting his investment. Reach in there and pull one out."

Ray reached into the stack and pulled out a tape. "I remember this one. I called it '4-giveness'—with the number four instead of the letters for four. I preached on forgiving others as Christ has forgiven you and I talked about four aspects of forgiveness."

"What were they?"

"What?"

"Your four aspects of forgiveness, what were they?"

"Oh. Well, Christ's forgiveness was *complete*. Um, it was *undeserved*. And it was…it was…two other things." Ray sighed. "And if I can't remember them, why would anyone else?"

"Now don't beat yourself up, Ray, that's not my point."

"No, I get it. Why give them four things when it's hard enough to remember one?"

"And remembering it isn't nearly as hard as applying it. If we give people three or four things to apply to their lives each week, they'll quit before they even begin."

"Okay, but how do you narrow it down, Will? I mean, when I'm studying and preparing, there's just so much."

"Now that's the huge upside to this whole approach."

"What's that, Will?"

"That tape you're holding would make an excellent four-part series called '4-giveness.' You see, studying and preparing a message is like looking up an address in the phone book or, for a guy your age, one of those online map things. You're going to see lots of other stuff, good stuff. Write it down and use it. Just don't use it all at one time in one message. There have been times that I couldn't wait to finish one message because I was so excited about a new insight. But you have to be disciplined. It's what I call the See Rock City trap."

"Rock City?"

"Yeah. It's a tourist attraction in Chattanooga, Tennessee. It used to be that everywhere you drove from north Georgia to the Carolinas and throughout Tennessee you'd see barns with "See Rock City" painted on the roof. Well, by the time you got to Chattanooga you just had to pull off and…"

"See Rock City," Ray finished the thought.

"Exactly. And insights can be the same way. You can be so excited by a different idea or another element of a passage that you forget where you're headed and start taking a side trip. It may be a great place, but it's not where you were going and you'll confuse your listeners."

Could that be the reason for those confused looks I've been seeing on Sunday mornings? Ray wondered. He couldn't help but laugh as he thought of how many series he had preached on one Sunday morning.

"Okay, Will. I can buy that it's much easier to remember one thing than three or four, but it's hard for me to envision talking about one thing for thirty or forty minutes."

"All depends. What's your goal?"

"So we're back to the goal thing again? In this case my goal is to not run out of things to say ten minutes after I start."

"Look, don't get hung up on how long it takes or doesn't take. Besides, I'm not saying to say the same thing over and over—like the number forty-four. I'm saying that every story, every illustration, every question raised and answered should point to THE point. You can be creative and funny and all those things people like. Just be certain it takes you where you want to go. Ray, I've driven some of the finest rigs you've ever seen. They've had everything from TVs to coffee makers and vibrating seats. And yet even with all the bells and whistles, if the truck isn't headed in the right direction, it won't get you where you want to go. See what I mean?"

"Loud and clear." Ray smiled. "But you've switched word pictures on me. First the sermon was a journey, now it's an eighteen-wheeler."

"Buddy, you'll find that great analogies are like great trucks: They all break down at some point."

Ray sat back and watched the countryside pass by. Had the blank stares he'd seen from the congregation been confusion instead of boredom? Had he been serving water from a fire hydrant? Maybe he'd been trying to cram more information in his messages in an attempt to fill time—or possibly to impress people. *But one point?* Could he preach an entire message around one point?

Ray broke the silence. "Will, just how many imperatives are there?"

"What's that, Ray?"

"You said, *Pick a Point* is the second imperative of communication you learned from driving a truck. I was wondering how many there are."

"Well, I don't know that I've actually counted them before. Let's see..." Will began to squint and mumble as he searched his memory banks. "Thirty or forty, I'd say."

Ray sat stunned. "Then I need more underwear," he said, referring to the small overnight bag in the truck.

Will began to laugh. "I'm just kidding, Ray. You've got plenty of underwear. There are only seven."

5

A MAP TO
REMEMBER

"Will, I have been wondering one thing."

"What's that?"

"I don't want you to take this wrong but…" Ray struggled to find the words.

"Spit it out, Ray. It takes a lot to hurt my feelings."

"Well, you said we were going to talk about how to be a better communicator and you haven't mentioned anything about God or prayer. Is this all about human effort?"

"Yes." Will said flatly.

Ray wasn't expecting that answer.

"Look, Ray," Will broke the silence, "neither you or I will ever have anything meaningful to say if God doesn't give it to us. The most important time you will spend in developing a message is the time you spend prayerfully searching the heart of God and His Word for your one point."

"Sounds like there's a 'but' coming."

"But, once God has done His part, we have to do our part. And I've heard far too many preachers hide behind the excuse that it's up to the

Holy Spirit to apply the message to the heart of the hearer and then not give the Holy Spirit anything to work with."

Satisfied that Will wasn't a self-help guru, Ray pressed on, "So what's the third imperative?"

"The third, which is near and dear to the heart of any trucker, is: *Create a Map.*"

Ray's idea of a good map was one that was easy to refold after he'd used it. "Okay, so what do you mean by a map? Obviously you're not talking about something I can pick up at Triple A."

Will laughed. "As a trucker I used a map as a two-dimensional picture of a three-dimensional journey. A good map will allow you to find the best and most effective course for arriving at your destination. Like I said when we were discussing the second imperative, there are a lot of different ways to get to a particular location. As a driver, I had to find the most effective route for getting my cargo to its destination at exactly the time it needed to be there.

"You see, a lot of folks think a good map shows you all the possible options all the time, but for me that's a *terrible* map. When I set out on a trip I'd take my road atlas and map out my course on a sheet of paper. *That* would be my map. The atlas would have thousands of other twists and turns that would only get me in trouble."

"And as a communicator you learned to narrow it down to one destination. Didn't we cover that already?"

"This is different, Ray. As a communicator, your goal is to get your audience to the final point of application. The map I'm talking about charts the course of your message."

"So you're talking about an outline," Ray said.

"No, I'm talking about a *map*. Outlines are designed to organize thoughts and ideas. They're usually a collection of points related to or loosely related to a topic—each one of those points making an entirely different statement about the topic."

"Like my outline for the forgiveness message," Ray said weakly.

"Exactly. You had a lot to say about forgiveness in your outline, but your outline didn't take you anywhere. It wasn't…"

"A map."

"Right! You see," Will continued, "outlines can end up being like an encyclopedia—lots of good information that's dry and boring. People rarely curl up in bed with an encyclopedia. A map on the other hand leads people on a journey that engages them into a story—just like the one you told me about your vacation."

Ray was trying hard to get it. "You keep saying 'map.' So how literally am I supposed to take this? You sit down with paper and, what, colored pencils and crayons, and draw stuff?"

Will glanced over at his passenger. "Do I look like the kind of guy who uses crayons, Ray?"

"Okay…so it's another analogy. So how do you draw this map?"

"Usually I sit at my desk with a piece of paper and start with Roman numeral one," Will said.

"It *is* an outline!" Ray said as if he'd caught the old man in a lie.

Will laughed. "Does it make you feel better to call it an outline, Ray?"

"It makes me feel better to know that I might be doing *something* right."

"Not so fast. Just because it looks like an outline, doesn't make it right. In my thinking there are two different kinds of outlines. One is informational and it's all about content. That's the kind of outline you work from. Four or five points that…"

"Okay, okay, I get the picture," Ray blurted out. "What's the other kind of outline?"

Will began to wonder if he was pushing Ray too hard. It had been a long day for him, even though it was only late afternoon. "Maybe we should find a place to stop and take a break for a while."

"I'm sorry, Will, I didn't mean to pop off. It's just that this is critical for me. I've given my life to this work and—to think that I've been doing it wrong all this time…" Ray's voice trailed off as he turned his face toward the window.

Will's voice softened a little. "You know, Ray, right and wrong are pretty harsh terms sometimes. I'm sorry if I've made you think that my way is the *right* way and all others are wrong. That's not at all what I mean. God has used you to build a successful ministry, and people have been touched through the years. Never doubt it! I'm just trying to offer you another option that's worked well for me and a few others. Would you like to stop for a while?"

Ray considered the question. Since he had no idea where they were headed, it was difficult to know if this was a good time to stop. "Will, just where are we going?"

"Oh, here and there. And if it's all the same to you, I'd like to keep going for a while. I know a spot up the road where we can pull off soon."

"You're the driver. But listen…I really do want to get this. What's the second type of outline you're talking about?"

"Well, if the first type is an informational outline," Will began, "the second type is what I call a *relational* outline. It's building your outline around the relationships between you the speaker, your audience, and then God, of course. I use the outline as a map to chart my course of interacting and interrelating between them. I call it ME-WE-GOD-YOU-WE."

"ME-WE… what?" Ray tried to repeat it back.

"ME-WE-GOD-YOU-WE."

"It sounds like the name of a summer camp," Ray joked. "Where'd you go last summer? Oh, I went to Camp Mewegoduwe."

Will laughed. "Well, I can't say it's as much fun as summer camp, but it is the route I take on my preaching journey." And with that Will launched into an explanation.

"The ME section—well, that's where you have to start. That's where you explain who you are and what you're all about. I've spoken in a lot of places to a lot of different groups, and the ME part is where I introduce myself to the folks. An audience needs a certain comfort level with a speaker before they'll really listen. A pastor speaking in his church doesn't need a lot of introduction, and he can use this time to introduce the idea or topic of the morning.

"You see, Ray, once I feel like my listeners know me a little and that they trust me, then I'm ready to engage them. We'll talk more about that in the next imperative, but for now, that's the purpose of the WE section. It takes me from what I'm thinking or feeling to what WE are thinking and feeling. I have to find an emotional common ground with them around the topic or idea of the message. I may say something like, 'As husbands we know this' or 'As fathers we know that,' and I've connected with another group. But I can't stop there. I have to move to other age groups and such until I feel like I've found as much common ground as I can with the audience. Make sense? My goal is to raise a felt need with as many people in the audience as I can.

"Once I've done that," Will went on, "I can move on my map to the next relationship, and that's with God. The GOD section of the map is where I take this emotional common ground I've established and introduce biblical truth into the discussion. Now I'm providing a solution to the need I just raised. A lot of the preachers I know feel like they have to start with Scripture and then offer an application."

"Guilty as charged," Ray said. "It's the way I was taught."

"The problem with that approach," Will caught himself, "or I should say, the *challenge* with that approach, is that you're simply teaching Scripture on an informational basis. If your audience doesn't feel the need to listen, then a lot of times they just won't. They might still be sitting there staring at you, but they will have tuned you out."

Ray nodded. He knew all too well what Will was talking about.

"Remember, Ray, we're not teaching the Bible to people; we're teaching *people* the Bible. First, we connect with the people; then we move to the Bible."

Ray thought about the faraway looks and near catatonic stares that often looked back at him from the auditorium. He knew his audience, and they knew him all too well. But had he taken the time to connect them with the truth of God's Word?

"That leads us to YOU." Will was on a roll now. "Once I've introduced God's view on the subject as the answer to the need, it makes it easy for me to then ask, 'What are you going to do about it?' This becomes the application segment. But if I've followed my map well, instead of having to stir up interest in making the application, the application comes as a relief." Will saw the look of disbelief in Ray's eyes. "Okay, it's not *always* a relief. But it's always the answer to a question they're already asking."

Ray felt like needling his mentor just a little. "This segment is called YOU. Does that mean the speaker is exempt from the application?"

"Aw, you know better than that, Ray. I call it YOU because I want to make sure I'm communicating the challenge at a personal level. You see, life change is going to come when people apply the truth to their lives—and they sure as anything *won't* apply it until they feel like they really need to."

"So at this point," Ray began, "you can go back and make application to the groups you addressed in the WE section."

"Bingo. That's right on, brother. The outline—I mean, map—gives you the groups you need to cover with your application. You just go back, and everywhere you raised a need, now you make an application. But that leads to an important point, Ray. Don't raise a felt need that you aren't going to cover from God's Word and answer with an application.

The worst thing a communicator can do is overpromise and under-deliver. You're building trust with your listeners. Not just trust in the information, but…"

"Trust in the relationship," Ray finished his thought. "What was the last word, Will, was it WE again?"

"That's right," Will said. "The last point on the relational map is WE. The earlier WE was a place to build common ground around a felt need. *This* WE is a place to cast a common vision."

"A vision?"

"A vision of what our lives, our church, and even our world would look like if only we would apply the truth of God's Word. It's the inspirational part of the message. My goal at this point is to inspire people to make a change. Sometimes being faced with God's Word can leave the listener feeling defeated, if all they think about is how far they have to go. But if I can give them a picture of what life will be like once they apply the truth, then they have a little hope."

"ME-WE-GOD-YOU-WE," Ray said. "Hey, I remembered! I think I can hold on to a map like that."

"And that's why it's such a good map to have, buddy. In imperative number two, when I said you have to pick a point and make it memorable, I told you that the right map would make that possible. And with this map…"

"I talk about *me* and the challenges *we* face," Ray began to complete Will's sentence like the question on a final exam. "Then I look at what *God* has said about it and the answers that He's given us. I offer personal application so that *you* can change your life and then how *we* can all celebrate that change together."

"And if at any time you get lost or confused, all you have to do is remember what relationship you're on, and then you know right where you're going," Will concluded.

As Ray mulled over these thoughts, it occurred to him that Will had never answered his question. "Will, you never did tell me where we're headed," Ray said.

"No, I didn't, did I?" Will smiled.

For the first time since his surreal adventure began, Ray began to review the facts. He didn't know where he was going with a man he had just been introduced to by another man he hardly knew. It should have been a little uncomfortable. But somehow, it wasn't.

Ray settled back into the large, comfortable seat of the oversized truck and smiled. He may not have known just where he was headed, but he knew it wasn't back to where he'd been.

6

LOAD UP BEFORE
YOU LEAVE

"So what's the fourth imperative?" Ray asked.

"The fourth is very dependent on the second and third. I call it *Internalize the Message*. You see, knowing your destination and then having a good map are just preparation for the journey. Before I ever headed off cross-country, I had to make certain I knew how to get there."

"Right. We just talked about having the right kind of map for the journey." Ray said.

"Yes, but having the map and *knowing* where I was going were two different things. Once I climbed behind the wheel of that truck, I needed to know how I was going to get to my destination. I couldn't be looking down at a map trying to figure out the best route or where to turn. That's how accidents happen. I needed to *know* the best highways. Besides knowing my route, I needed to know my cargo, when my shipment was due, and a few other things to be ready for the trip. Driving long haul can take a lot out of you, and so you need to make sure you're ready before you begin. In other words, I needed to load up."

Ray could tell just by looking at Will that he would never leave home without being ready. He had the look of a man who was ready for just about anything. "How did that make you a better communicator?" Ray asked.

"I learned that I didn't want to step up in front of that crowd until I was ready. I had to *load up* to say something."

Ray looked out the window. *Was this really something new? Didn't every communicator know not to stand up until he had something to say?*

"What is it?" Will asked.

"I dunno. I guess the 'load up' thing seems pretty obvious."

"You'd think so, wouldn't you? But I've seen a lot of preachers and speakers stand up and deliver a talk like they're reading the phone book."

"Oh, you're talking about delivery style," Ray said.

"No," the older man replied, "it's far more than that. I've heard guys preach messages and I would swear it was the first time they'd ever seen the words. I'm talking about internalizing a message until it's a part of you and you own it. In the old days, preachers called it their "burden." It's a message that comes from inside you, and then you stand up and deliver it."

"Are you saying to deliver it with no notes, from memory?"

"I'm saying that until you *can* deliver it with no notes, from memory, then it's not your message. You may know where you want to go, but you haven't internalized the way to get there."

"Will, I've tried to memorize my messages before, and I just can't. I get confused on how to say something, and then I get flustered and completely lost." Ray's voice reflected frustrated experience.

"Do you have kids, Ray?" Will asked.

"What? Uh, yeah, I have two."

"Do you like to travel? Go on family vacations?" Will was making a point, but Ray wasn't sure yet what it was—or what it had to do with what they had just been talking about.

"When we get the chance," Ray said cautiously. "What are you getting at?"

Will ignored the question. "Tell me about your favorite trip and why it's your favorite."

Ray shrugged and launched into his story. "I guess my favorite trip was one we took a couple of years ago. My wife, Sally, and I took our kids back to where I grew up. My folks don't live there anymore, so we really had no good reason to go back. It had been a while since I'd taken some time off, so we had plenty of vacation saved up. We were able to take three weeks and stay on the back roads, and I really got to show my kids where I spent time when I was their age."

Over the next few minutes, Ray unfolded the story of his journey. He had Will alternating between laughter, as he told of his first girlfriend and poorly aimed first kiss, and tears as he spoke of the trip to his grandfather's gravesite and the impact the old man had on Ray's life. As Ray finished his tale he concluded by saying, "I guess the best part of the trip was what I saw in my kids' eyes. They finally saw that I was once a kid with all the same hopes and fears they have. In a lot of ways, it opened doors for me to their hearts."

"That's a great message, Ray. Can I get a copy of your notes?"

"Notes? You know there aren't any notes."

"Amazing. And yet you seemed to have no problem remembering. You not only got all the facts right, but you organized them well and made me laugh and cry. I even learned an insight about being a dad."

"But that's different, Will. I wasn't preaching. I was just telling a story."

"And in that one statement you've unlocked the secret of *Internalize the Message*," Will responded. "Until you can stand up and tell a story, you're not ready to preach. You see, people connect with a story, and a story takes people on a journey. Whether it's a journey to your childhood home or a journey to a life-changing truth, it's a story that will take you there. And did you notice how effortlessly you told it? You didn't stumble over words. You didn't forget major elements, but you obviously left out unimportant details."

"Like what?"

"Well, I heard all about a great road trip and yet have no idea what kind of vehicle you drive. It was important on your trip, but not to the story."

"I get it," Ray said. "And it was a minivan." Ray wasn't sure, but he thought he saw a flash of disdain on Will's face at the mention of a minivan. But he was a trucker, after all.

"You see, Ray, speaking from memory isn't difficult to do if you're telling a story. People make it difficult when they try to communicate points instead of telling a story. If you have four or five points you're trying to drive home, then you get focused on not forgetting any of them."

"So that's why it's important to have a one point message. That way you only have one thing to remember," Ray said.

"Pete said you were a quick learner! Obviously there are more things to remember than the main point, but far fewer than most preachers think. When I leave for a long trip I not only know where I want to end up, but I know the major roads I need to take. I've committed the route to memory, and so when I get to the road, I take it. My job depended on me knowing that route. Most preachers I've watched don't act like anything is dependent on them knowing where they're going."

"I hate to show you that I'm not as quick as you think I am, Will. But what is dependent on it?"

"How can you expect your listener to care enough to remember what you're saying when you can't?" Will let the words sink in.

"I never thought of it that way," Ray said.

Will continued. "When you stand up and speak without notes and

without having to read your sermon, you're saying, 'This is so important that it's a part of me—and I think you should make it a part of you,
too.'"

"Will," Ray began, "when I think about the messages I usually
preach, I can't *imagine* doing it without any notes! It's hard enough
sometimes with the outline sitting right in front of me."

Will smiled. "That's because you've always used an outline. Now
you have a good map."

7

CRUCIAL
CONNECTIONS

"Well, Ray, I'm guessing that the lunch you had with Pete this afternoon is pretty much history. You could probably use a little dinner."

Food. The day had been such a whirlwind that it hadn't dawned on Ray that it had been several hours—and many miles—since he last ate. "Now that you mention it, I could stand a bite or two. Are we going to one of those greasy spoon diners that truckers always eat in?"

Will smiled. "You watch too much television, Ray. One of the benefits of retiring from the road is that you have time to eat in better places. But don't knock a truck stop until you've tried it. I'd take good diner coffee anytime over one of those fancy *latte* places. Anyhow, I know a great steak house up the road. There's a guy there I want you to meet. As for where we're headed...well, we'll make a couple of stops here and there, but the cab of this truck is pretty much our destination. Pete thought you would benefit from our spending some time together and, for some crazy reason, I just seem to think better behind the wheel of a truck." And just maybe, some things would be easier said looking straight ahead than face-to-face.

The steak house was a welcome sight for both men as Will wheeled into the parking lot. The place was crowded, which Ray took as a good sign of things to come. The two men were shown to their seats and both ordered the New York strip.

"Well, if that's my salad on its way over here, then I'm ready for the fourth imperative," Ray said.

After the waitress delivered the salads, Will offered a short blessing for the food. Looking up, he gestured with his fork and said, "*Engage the Audience.*"

"Beg your pardon?"

"That's it. That's the fifth one. Every truck driver worth his salt knows to secure his load."

"You mean, tie things down?" Ray asked.

"Not just tie them down. It's more than that." Will spoke between mouthfuls of salad and bread. "When I back a tractor up to 9,000 gallons of gasoline, I want to know that it's going to stay with me. Know what I mean?"

Ray nodded.

"First of all," Will continued, "it's my job—my responsibility—to get the load to its destination. And second, it could get dangerous if things broke loose. Now bring that over to our discussion. As a communicator, I have to be just as certain that I've secured my cargo."

"And securing your cargo is the same as really knowing your main point, right?" Ray was pleased with himself for tracking so well.

"Nice try, Ray. The main point is your destination. But in this case, your cargo is your audience. That's why you have to *engage the audience.* As a communicator, you can know exactly where you're going, but if you head off in a cloud of dust and leave your audience behind, it won't matter if you get there or not. You have to *engage* your listeners and make certain that they're with you. This is the first WE section on the message map. As a trucker, I had to make sure that the trailer was engaged. Once it was locked down I was good to go. When I'm preaching, I have to engage with my audience on an emotional level and then I know they're on board with me."

"An emotional level?" Ray asked. "You're not a crier, are you Will?"

"Do I look like a crier?" Will asked mildly, attacking his dinner roll with a butter knife.

No, Will certainly did not look like a crier.

"Okay, then. What do you mean 'on an emotional level'?"

"You have to connect with your audience around a real need in their lives. Something they *feel*. You have to raise in them an awareness of a past, present, or future need in their lives that makes them want to listen to you and follow you to the answer. It's not enough to say, 'I have the truth of God's Word up here and it's your job to listen.' That might have worked years ago, but not today. No way. Today you have to show people how the truth impacts their lives."

"But isn't my job to preach the Word of God and allow Him to use it as He sees fit?" Ray asked. "What if my text for the day doesn't address a felt need as much as it addresses something we *need* to do—like pray, for instance. I don't think many of my listeners have a felt need to pray."

"But they do have a felt need for guidance, for peace, to know God's will in troubled times," Will answered. "Can you meet those needs without prayer?"

"No," Ray said quietly. "No, you really can't. No one can."

As these thoughts sunk in, the waitress delivered the rest of the meal. Two steaks with baked potatoes and the works. The two hungry men dove into the food as if it had been days, not hours, since their last meal. After getting a start on the food, Will finally spoke.

"Ray, I'm not saying we ought to water down the message. Not at all! I'm saying that we take the life-changing truth and make very sure we apply it to lives that are ready to be changed. It's just that we may have to remind them that they *want* to change."

"How?" Ray asked. How do we make them feel it?"

"Tension," Will responded. "We create tension."

"Look, I know I'm not the expert here. But I've been around ministry long enough to know that our job is to *relieve* tension, not create it."

Will laughed. "You may be right. But it's not so much that I create tension; it's that I remind them of the tension they already feel. The tension of trying to be the kind of husbands or wives or parents they're supposed to be. I challenge them to look at the weaknesses in their lives and ask the question, 'Then what do I do about it?' If I can get them there, then I'm halfway home. Once I get them wanting to know the answer, then I know I have 'em until the end of the message. I've secured my cargo and I don't have to worry about losing it."

"No, but you'd better deliver when you get them to the end," Ray said.

"You're so right. That's why we're talking about engaging your audience. Another way you can hold an audience is to get them to look at things in a way they've never looked at them before. There's someone I want you to meet."

With that Will left the table, returning shortly with another man. "Ray, this is Larry Wayne. He owns this fine establishment." Larry Wayne was about Will's age, but his waistline made it obvious that he had enjoyed the work of his chef.

"Nice to meet you, Ray," Larry said. "Any friend of Will's is a friend of mine."

"Larry built this place a few years back, but for thirty years he worked the lounges in Vegas, Reno, and Atlantic City." Ray's eyes lit up as he heard this. "Anytime I was driving through a town he was playing, I'd make sure I stopped to see him."

"Are you a singer?" Ray asked.

"What?" Larry joked. "I don't look like a dancer? Just kidding, Ray. I do stand-up."

"Larry was one of the best stand-up comedians on the circuit. I wanted you to meet him, because if anyone can connect with an audience, it's Larry."

"So are you a performer, Ray?" Larry asked.

"Me? Oh no, I'm not a performer. I'm in the ministry," Ray said almost apologetically. It was a topic Ray always dreaded. Anytime he told someone what he did, he always felt like they pigeonholed him as "a religious person."

"Hey, that's great," Larry said. "Will led me to Christ twenty years ago. That's why his money is never good in my place."

"And why I always order the best steak in the joint," Will replied with a smile.

"But listen, Ray," Larry said, "don't kid yourself about not being a performer. If you're a preacher, then you're a performer just like me. The sooner you accept it, the better off you'll be."

"Why do you say that?"

"Well, we both make our living trying to convince a group of people that they're glad they came out to hear us," Larry said.

"I guess I never thought of it that way."

"You really need to learn to think like a comedian, Ray," Will said.

"You want me to tell jokes?" Ray asked.

"Only if you're funny!" Larry laughed. "But seriously, it's not that you need to tell jokes. Some people are really good at that, and other people are like Will here."

"Hey, I didn't come here to be insulted."

"No, you just came to eat my steak. Ray, you need to become an observer of people and situations. Whenever I stand up in front of a crowd, I'm constantly looking for ways to connect with them. It could be the weather that day or something in the news, or even a funny hat that some lady is wearing. Anything that can help me make that first connection. When it's your regular crowd, you're already connected so you can move right to the issue."

"Anything to make ME into WE," Ray said, looking at Will.

"Exactly. Your goal is to *connect*. Another thing that I learned from watching comedians like Larry was the benefit of being a skeptic."

"A skeptic?"

Larry sat down and began to talk with Ray. "You see, a skeptic questions the status quo. They look at things differently from everyone else. As a comedian, my job is to look at things and to get my audience to look at things in ways they never have before. I get them to see the humor in the mundane things of life. Your job is to look at the truth of Scripture from every point of view: the believer and the unbeliever, men and women, young and old. Once you've done that, you can ask and answer the questions that your audience is asking. Then you've connected. You see, Ray, we're all in the connecting business. We engage for different purposes, but ultimately our success comes down to whether or not the people are with us. For me there were only a few laughs at stake, but for you the stakes are much higher."

Ray sat and listened as Will and Larry reminisced about the old days in Vegas and Atlantic City. Secretly, Ray wished he had a tape recorder because some of these stories were great illustrations. As the evening drew to a close Larry was good to his word, allowing no check to be delivered to the table. Will and Ray left the restaurant, climbed back into the cab of the truck and headed out onto the highway.

As the two drove in silence, the big meal began to have an effect. It was getting late and Ray was in serious need of sleep. "So, are we driving all night or does this thing have a pop-up camper in it somewhere?"

"Are you ready for some shut-eye, Ray?"

"I could use a little if there's a good hotel around here."

With that Will jerked the wheel of the truck so violently that it threw Ray against the passenger door. His head hit the window with a thud and the tires squealed as the truck swerved onto an exit ramp.

Stunned by the abrupt actions of the normally careful driver, Ray practically shouted, "Will, what in heaven's name are you doing?"

Will just looked ahead and said, "One last point for imperative number five, my boy."

"Number five?" Ray said. "After that bump on my head I'll be lucky if I can remember my name, much less five imperatives."

"Aw c'mon. You're being a little dramatic, aren't you? Besides I'm old enough to be your father, and I didn't hit *my* head."

Ray couldn't believe Will's attitude. What had happened to the kind old truck driver from Atlanta? In all honesty, Ray had to admit that Will's sudden actions had startled more than injured him. The truck exited the highway and pulled into the parking lot of a hotel.

"Does this place look alright to you?"

"The hotel is fine but the knot on my head needs an explanation."

"An explanation? Well, since I was driving I assumed it was up to me to get us to a hotel. Besides, like I said, I'm older than you and I didn't hit my head."

"That's because you knew where we were going! You were ready for the turn and I wasn't."

"Funny how that works, isn't it?"

"Okay, I'm supposed to get some kind of point here, right? Look, Will, I know you're getting at something that has to do with communication and driving and a journey and probably stand-up comedy, too, but I haven't slept in…"

"Okay, fair enough. You made a great statement a minute ago, Ray."

"I did?"

"Uh-huh. And it would help every communicator to remember it."

"I'm guessing it wasn't about the bump on my head."

"Not directly. And, well, I am sorry about that part of it. It wasn't supposed to happen quite like that. I was just trying to make a memorable point."

Ray admitted that his head was fine and that whatever Will's point was, he was sure he'd never forget it.

Will continued. "A few minutes ago you pointed out that the reason I didn't hit my head on that sharp turn was because I knew where we were going. I was ready for it. As a truck driver—or a driver of any kind, for that matter—there will always be times when people follow us. Sometimes they're following us on purpose to get somewhere, and sometimes they just happen to be behind us on the road. Either way, these folks have no idea when we're about to turn or change directions. It's up to us to stay aware of that."

"Okay," Ray replied, "then what are you supposed to do?"

"I'll send that question right back to you. What do *you* do when someone is following you and you're about to make a turn?"

"Use my turn signals. And then I slow down, glancing in my rearview mirror to make sure they're still with me."

"That's exactly right, Ray," Will said with a smile. "Part of keeping your audience engaged is taking it slow in the turns."

"To be honest, that's what went through my mind just after my head hit your window. *Why didn't he slow down and let me know he was turning?*"

"Right. Good question. Now bring it over into the realm of speaking and preaching. As a communicator, you're the only one in the room who knows in advance where you're going on the journey. You're the leader and everyone looks to you for the signals. Remember, Ray, when you put together a sermon you're really mapping out the journey—and every journey has twists and turns. But it also has mile markers to indicate where the turns need to happen. These are the points of transition, from ME to WE, and WE to GOD, and so on in the message map.

"In a sermon, you and I call these *transitions*, in which we move from one aspect of the message to another. When you come to one of these points you have the option of taking an abrupt turn like I did earlier, or of giving your listeners verbal and nonverbal clues that a transition is coming."

"And if my experience is any indicator, it's probably a good idea to let them know what's coming." Ray rubbed the sore spot on his head.

"It could've been worse," Will said. "I've seen some guys make such hard turns in a message that they threw people right out the door and they never came back."

"What are the signals, Will? Should I install blinkers on my pulpit?"

"If you're still using a pulpit, you might need to."

"Do you have something against pulpits?"

"No, not really, I... Okay, I *do* have something against them. I think they have the tendency to isolate the communicator from the audience—and they limit your ability to use the space to your advantage."

"What space?"

"Exactly!" Will said. "The pulpit usually takes up all the space on the platform, and you have no room to move around. Physical, nonverbal cues can be useful indicators to people that you are transitioning. You can move to a certain spot and let it represent a new idea. If you spend all of your time standing behind a pulpit looking down at notes, you lose that ability—and you forfeit that option."

"Which goes back to *Internalize the Message*," Ray offered.

"You're exactly right. But what good does it do to internalize a message and then hide behind a pulpit?"

"I guess I never thought of it as hiding."

"No," Will said, "but you have to admit, it does give the impression that you're separated from the people. These are just the nonverbal indicators. More important are the verbal clues we give people to let them know it's time to transition. In the old days guys would just say, 'The second point is...,' as if they were reading a term paper."

Ray smiled, not wanting to tell Will that the "old days" were last week's sermon. Ray remembered clicking quickly through four points in his message. He hadn't considered transitions all that important. That's what he'd always thought fill-in-the-blank sermon notes were for.

"Okay, no blinkers on the pulpit. And no pulpit! What are the best ways to give a verbal indication?" Ray asked.

"You want to carefully craft a transitional statement to get you from one section of your map to another," Will replied.

"Give me an example."

"Well, if I'm moving from the WE section to the GOD section, I may say something like, 'Isn't it great to know that even though we all face this issue, God's Word has something to say about it?' That's pretty simple, and I would usually do more. But at least I've tied the tension to the next section in the Scripture."

Ray took all of this in. *How many times have I knocked heads against windows or possibly thrown people right out of the sanctuary?* Truth be told, though, the idea of throwing a few people out of the sanctuary didn't sound all that bad.

"You know, Ray, this also applies to the entire worship service. I can't tell you how many services I've been to where the music, the announcements, the message, and the other elements seem disjointed. A little attention to transitional statements or music that's chosen because of what came before or after can make the service feel more like a moment to be experienced, instead of various moments to be endured."

Ray sat back in the comfortable bucket seat and thought. "So let me see if I have this," he finally said. "If you use your turn signals, you'll make transitions that will take people to the next mile marker on the journey, instead of leaving them on the side of the road. And that will help me keep my audience engaged. Does that sound about right?"

"Sounds good to me," Will said. "And if this hotel is okay with you then this is a good place to stop for the night."

Ray and Will checked in and, before heading off to his room, Will shouted back to Ray, "Breakfast is at 7:30 a.m. *sharp*. Don't be late."

Will's tone momentarily made Ray consider sleeping in the cab of the truck but in a matter of moments Ray was lying in a comfortable bed in room 108. He picked up the phone and called Sally to fill her in on his amazing journey. He told her all about Will and the seven imperatives—or at least the five he knew at this point. He assured her that he would be home tomorrow, but in the back of his mind he wasn't all that certain. After the second round of "good night" and "I love you," Ray set the alarm and fell asleep.

8

SHOW ME SOME IDENTIFICATION

Ray slept better than he had in a long time. *Maybe there is light at the end of this preaching tunnel.* He and Will were on the road in no time at all and in search of breakfast. The drive-through service was fast and friendly and once again they were on their way.

"How's the coffee?" Will asked. Ray nodded approvingly. "Those drive-through windows are the best thing that ever happened to hauling. You can make up a lot of time when you don't have to stop."

"Speaking of stopping, Will, we're five imperatives down and two to go, so don't stop now."

"Don't you want to finish your breakfast first?"

"I'm a multitasker."

"Well, Ray, the next imperative is one that you shouldn't have a problem with..."

"Well it's about time!" Ray interrupted.

"You shouldn't, but you do."

"Oh great."

"Ray, do you see that truck over there?" Will pointed at a huge rig on the northbound side of the interstate.

Ray looked across the median and saw the large white eighteen-wheeler pulling a trailer. "Yeah, it's hard to miss something that big."

"That's a Peterbilt 379 EXHD. Just a minute ago we passed a Volvo WG64T and, before that, a Mack CH6113—"

Ray interrupted again, "So is this imperative some kind of "Rainman" gift for identifying big rigs?"

Will laughed. "No, that's not it. But that *is* a good example of what I'm talking about."

"An example of what?"

"Imperative number six is *Find Your Voice*," Will said. "For forty years I was a Kenworth man. I drove a lot of different models in a lot of different colors, but they were all Kenworths. And as a Kenworth man, I wouldn't consider driving a Mack or a Volvo—or any other truck for that matter. Nothing wrong with those other rigs. In fact, some of them had some nice features. It's just that, I was a Kenworth man and that's the way it was."

"You sound like some of my NASCAR friends who argue over Ford versus Chevy."

"Same thing. A Chevy man wouldn't be caught dead in a Ford, and vice versa."

"I see."

"Really?"

"No, I'm lying. I don't have a clue what this has to do with anything, but it's interesting—in a primal, truck driver sort of way. Although, for some reason, I feel like I should be eating some red meat with my fingers."

Will laughed. "There it is again."

Ray looked up. "What, another truck?"

"No, Ray, your sense of humor. You're really a funny guy. Part of your voice is your humor. The problem is, I never knew that about you."

Ray gave Will a confused look. "Maybe I'm missing something, but didn't we just meet yesterday?"

"Not really." Once again Will reached over and opened the glove box on the dashboard. He reached in and grabbed a handful of cassettes. "You forget, Ray, that I've known you a lot longer than you've known me."

"Yeah, Will, but those aren't *me*; those are my sermons." As the words came out of his mouth, Ray realized what he was saying. "I mean, those are a part of me, of course, it's just that…what I'm saying is that listening to a sermon isn't like talking to a person."

"If you weren't talking to people, just who or what were you talking to?"

"Of course I was talking to people. But it's *preaching*…you know," Ray was struggling to explain something that he thought was universally understood.

"You weren't talking *to* people, Ray. You were talking *at* people. And there's a big difference." Will seemed intent on the road ahead, obviously avoiding eye contact. "What's worse is that it's not even *you* talking at the people. It's some other guy who's very serious—all business—and has no sense of humor at all. Shoot, Ray, your *voice* is even different. I can't tell you how pleasantly surprised I was when I met you. After listening to your messages, I wasn't sure if I wanted to spend a couple of hours with you, much less a couple of days."

Ray's mind was spinning. *When Will decides to back up his truck and dump it, he doesn't hold back. Could all of this be true? Have I been talking at people? Of course I was talking at people. I was preaching! Preachers talk at people. That's what they do. They have for centuries. It's the natural order of things, and who is this truck driver who thinks he can mess with that?* Ray was having an argument with himself, and doing quite well until Will broke in.

"Ray? You still with me?"

"I dunno, Will. I think I am but—this could be someone else speaking and I only *think* I'm here." Obviously Ray's feelings were still hurt.

"Look, I told you some of this wasn't gonna be easy."

"I thought you meant learning some kind of new study technique, not learning to be someone I'm not."

"That's just it, Ray—you've *already* learned to be someone you're not! I want you to be who you *are*. I want you to drive the truck you were born to drive; to *Find Your Voice*. I want you to stand up in front of your people and be YOU. It's as simple as that. You're a funny man. You're warm and friendly with an amazingly quick wit. You obviously care a great deal for people, and I know you have a lot to offer."

Ray wasn't sure if a hug was coming, but at the moment he was grateful for the console between him and Will. He knew Will was right. The problem was, he didn't know what to do about it. He had come to Will to find out what to do, and now the answer was to be himself?

"Wait a minute," Ray said, "if I'm supposed to be me, why am I here learning how you communicate?"

"That's a valid question. My goal wasn't to give you a speaking style or for you to become a clone of me. My goal was to give you a few things that will allow you to be who you are when you communicate. That's the beauty of taking people on a journey instead of giving them a sermon."

"Yeah. Okay. I get it...I guess."

"Do you remember earlier when you told me about your vacation?" Ray nodded. "That was a *story*—and a good one. You told it well. It was interesting and funny and even pretty touching in places. You held my attention the whole time. You do know how to tell a good story, Ray. All you have to do is stand up and tell a story as yourself. Most of the time you seem to be preaching in the third person. You talk about things that happen to other people and things other people have said. That's one of the problems when people manuscript a message: It sounds like they're reading something because, well, they *are* reading something. Your congregation needs to hear you *talk to them*."

"I know I keep asking the same question, but *how*, Will?"

"You and I have sat in this truck for the past two days and carried on a conversation. You need to carry on a conversation with your people. You need to pull up a chair and discuss the various topics that you want to cover."

"But conversations are two-way," Ray pushed back. "Am I supposed to open up the floor for questions and comments?"

"Well, that would certainly be engaging," Will said, "but I wouldn't recommend it. You can carry on a conversation by asking the questions your audience would ask and then answering them. It's not that you ask them to talk; it's that you acknowledge they're *there*. We've covered this under ME-WE-GOD-YOU-WE. I just want you to believe that you can follow that map as yourself, not as me or as any other communicator."

"Another communicator?" Ray asked.

"Ray, one of the problems that a lot of communicators have is that they listen to the same preachers all the time. They have their favorites and listen to them so much that they begin to sound like them—Chuck Swindoll, Charles Stanley, Rob Bell—you name it. The truth is, you need to listen to a lot of different men and women. Not only to be exposed to different ideas, but so you won't be overly influenced by one particular style. Remember, the goal is to be *you* up there."

Will paused, glancing over at the young pastor. "However, there is one communicator that I want you to listen to as much as possible."

Ray's mind quickly raced through the pantheon of golden-throated orators. Who could he mean? Was there one example out there for all to follow?

"The communicator that you must listen to is *you*," Will said.

Pete put you up to this, Ray thought, as he remembered the admonishment to *Work on It* by listening to his own messages.

Will continued. "You're going to have to listen to every message. And you have to listen critically and carefully until you find your voice."

"When you say my voice, you mean my style?"

"I mean, until you and everyone else listening recognizes that you are you. And then once you find it, you have to keep listening to make sure you don't lose it. Also, if you can set up a video camera, that's even better. You'd be surprised how much you can learn by watching yourself speak."

"I just don't know, Will. I agree with you on this stuff, I just…I just don't know how to *start*. I've been doing this so long that I don't know if I even *can* change."

"I don't want to sound like a broken record here, but you change every Sunday when you walk onto that platform. You enter the church as you, and then when you get behind your pulpit you're…someone else. I'm trying to get you *not* to change. I'm trying to get you to stay you. But I know what you mean about getting started. I can give you something to try, but it's pretty radical."

"More radical than flying a thousand miles to learn to preach from a truck driver?"

"Maybe. I want you to close your eyes and think about the one spot on earth where you're most comfortable. The spot where you are most able to be you."

Ray closed his eyes. "I don't know. I guess it would be a swing in my backyard that my wife and I sit in."

"A swing, huh? Well, I was hoping you had a favorite chair or recliner, but if it's a swing, then a swing it is."

"What are you getting at?"

Will glanced at the younger man. "I told you it's radical. But I think you ought to get rid of your pulpit and set up a swing on your platform."

"*A swing?* On the platform?" Ray could only stare at his mentor. "I think you've spent too much time around gasoline fumes, Will."

"Maybe." Will began, "but you're gonna *have* to get comfortable up there, Ray, and one way to do that is to change the environment. I'm just glad you didn't say you were most comfortable in the bathroom."

Ray laughed out loud. "That would certainly be memorable! So *Find Your Voice* is all about being myself while I'm preaching. I guess I'd better find out if I'm a Kenworth or a Peterbilt man."

"Not liking trucks at all is an option. Not a very godly one, maybe, but it is an option."

9

STUCK IN THE MIDDLE OF NOWHERE

As the idea of finding his own voice settled in, Ray watched the countryside roll by. Everything Will had said made sense. For the first time in a long time Ray felt like he had a plan for communicating. The growing sense of confidence made the sudden wave of panic even more striking, *What if none of this works?*

"Will?" Ray asked tentatively. "Does this stuff ever fail?"

"What do you mean, Ray?"

"I mean, do these seven imperatives ever let you down?"

"If you're asking me if there are still times that I get stuck and don't know what I'm supposed to talk about, then the answer is yes."

"Great!" Ray said as the panic took full bloom.

"That's where number seven comes in."

"Number seven?" Ray asked. "That's right we've only covered six."

"And number seven is the last imperative that I learned from driving a truck. You see, as a driver your reputation is built on making your delivery on time. You can't be late or they won't have what they need when they need it. If a customer can't count on you to be on schedule and have their shipment on time…well, let's just say you won't be in business very long. Every time I climbed behind the wheel I knew that the time was coming when someone would be counting on my delivery. I also knew that there were a lot of things out there that could stand between me and that delivery; weather, traffic, bad drivers, and worst of all, equipment failure. I couldn't spend time spinning my wheels so I had to be ready for anything."

"Sounds like you should have been a postman, Will."

"Same principle, smaller truck," Will smiled. "The point is I had to make sure I had the right tools when I needed them."

Will pulled the truck off of the highway into a rest area and got out of the cab. Ray followed him to the rear of the truck where Will opened a large toolbox.

"This is small-time compared to what I used to carry on the road. I'd carry tools, flares, warning markers, a winch, anything I might need in case I got stuck."

"This is very educational and I'm definitely going to buy some of those flares when I get home, but what exactly does all of this have to do with communicating?"

"Every Sunday morning you have a delivery to make. And as far as I know Sundays come every seven days like it or not."

"Sometimes it feels like they come every three days, but go ahead."

"And on those Saturday nights when you're sitting there without a clear idea of where your message is going, you're stuck."

Ray thought for a moment. "I don't think I understand, Will. There have been times when I didn't like what I had to say, or had to find more to say, but I don't know that I've ever felt stuck. Lost, but not stuck."

"Lost and stuck are somewhat similar. Lost is when you don't know where you are going…"

"And we covered that, in *Pick a Point* and *Create a Map*, right?"

"Right," Will was impressed. "But stuck is when you know where you want to go but you don't seem to be able to get there. The reason you never felt stuck is because you weren't trying to get anywhere, you were just filling the time." Will could tell that this hit harder than he meant for it to.

Ray realized that this one point message process could be more difficult than he first thought. "I thought this was supposed to make communication easier, not harder."

"It makes it more effective, Ray. I never said anything about making it easier," Will laughed. "Don't worry, Ray, I'm just saying that if you practice the first six imperatives and really try to take your listeners on a journey to one point, there are going to be times that you get stuck. That's when you need number seven. Trust me, I know."

"So what's the magic number seven for when you get stuck?"

"*Find Some Traction*," Will answered. "When you get stuck you have to get started again."

"And what do you use to do that?"

"I go to the toolbox and pull out what I need."

"So I should light a flare on the pulpit? That should wake 'em up in the back row."

"Right idea, wrong toolbox," Will said. "I have two surefire tools for when I get stuck as a communicator. The first one is prayer."

"I was wondering when you were going to get around to praying."

"Ray, I never meant to give you the impression that this entire process wasn't covered in prayer. If you don't pray before, during, and after your preparation then you might as well not start at all. What I'm talking about here is getting on my face before God and allowing Him to check my alignment. Am I headed in the wrong direction? Is there something going on in me that needs to be fixed? Is there a flaw in the point I've picked?"

"I understand, Will. I didn't mean to imply that you weren't seeking God through all of this. So what's the second tool?"

"It's a checklist. A list of questions that help me evaluate if I'm on the right path for the journey and then for helping me get started again. I sit back and ask myself these questions and they help me gain traction."

"Are these trucker questions with CB lingo like 'Breaker breaker, Will, what's your 20?' You know, your location?"

Will didn't smile. "I know what 'your 20' means and CB's are no laughing matter. Since *Smokey and the Bandit* you civilians almost ruined the things. Thank God for the cell phone is all I can say."

"Sorry. Does that mean you aren't going to tell me the questions?"

Once again the smile returned to Will's face. "I'm going to tell you, Ray, but first get back in the truck. We have a schedule to keep."

The two men climbed back in and in no time were cruising back down the highway. "The questions are these," Will said. "What do they need to know? Why do they need to know it? What do they need to do? Why do they need to do it?"

"That's it?" Ray asked.

"That's a lot," Will responded. "After you spend the time you need studying the passage, it's easy to lose sight of the point you want to make while you're putting together your message. You get off on a tangent or an idea that's taking you in another direction."

"Rock City, right?"

"Exactly. And before you know it you're stuck in a cul de sac with no way to turn around. What do they need to know is about information. It's the biblical principle that you've carved out of Scripture. If at this point you can't articulate that point then you know where you need traction. Why do they need to know it is all about motivation. Have you given them a reason to apply this point to their daily lives? Then comes what do they need to do, which is obviously about application. Have you given them a way to apply it to their daily lives? And finally, why do they need to do it? And that one is all about inspiration. Giving them a vision of what their lives will look like once they've applied it. Once you've answered these questions, you'll be back on the road in no time."

"Again, Will, I don't want to seem disrespectful but that seems kind of obvious and simple."

Will didn't respond but quietly reached across the console separating he and Ray and reached into the glove box. He pulled out a shiny chrome crescent wrench. "Have you ever seen a tool that was more plain and simple than that, Ray?" Ray shook his head. "But I guarantee you that when it comes to loosening or tightening a bolt there's nothing better. Just because it's simple doesn't mean it's not effective. The best tools are."

10

A NEW ATTITUDE

As the two men continued down the highway, Ray noticed traffic beginning to increase, signaling an approach to a metropolitan area. A road sign confirmed his suspicion: *Atlanta, 14 miles.*

Ray and Will's excellent adventure was almost over as they returned to the point where it all began. Ray began to wonder if he would return to the same place as well. Can a tiger change his stripes? More pointedly, can a preacher change the way he's been preaching for years? Had all of this been for nothing or…was it possible that his people were in for a big surprise come Sunday morning?

Suddenly it hit Ray. The goal; Will never told him the real goal. "You've gotta tell me the goal, Will."

"What?"

"When we first started out you said it wasn't important that I know the goal just that I know I didn't know it. Well, we're getting close to the airport, and I think it's really important now."

"Ray, it's like those red shoes that girl wore in the Wizard of Oz, you've known the goal all along."

"There's no place like home?"

Will laughed. "No. It's so simple that you're not seeing it, Ray. Close your eyes and think about the people at Meadowland Community Church. What do you want for them?"

Ray closed his eyes and began to think through the faces of the men, women, and children of his church. He thought about the many conversations, counseling appointments, and stories he had heard over the past ten years. Stories of struggles and challenges, along with a few successes and changed lives. *Changed lives. That's it.* "I want to see their lives changed to reflect the love of Christ."

"See, it wasn't that hard, was it? Now that you've determined your goal, go take a single point of Scripture and present it in a clear, engaging, memorable way that they can apply and then watch God change their lives."

"Before yesterday I would've said, 'That's easy for you to say.' But as strange as the circumstances have been, I want you to know that I think you might have helped me."

Will could tell that something was bothering Ray. "You sound a little uncertain."

"Uncertain?" Ray laughed. "Will, I've been in ministry for ten years. And for ten years I've been doing things the only way I knew how. The way I was taught and the way I saw others do them before me. And now, in six months' time, after a night at a baseball game and a day in your truck, I'm thinking about launching out in a completely new direction. 'Uncertain' is putting it mildly."

The two men rode in silence as they turned into the Peachtree Dekalb Airport. The commuter airport was relatively quiet for midday. Will parked the truck and turned to Ray. "Does that scare you?" he asked.

"What?"

"Doing things in a completely new way."

"Shouldn't it?"

"I'd be worried about you if it didn't. But, Ray, there are two things that I want you to remember. First, God has given you a lot to say. I've listened to your tapes and you have great insight into His word. I really mean that. I believe that He wants to impact a lot of lives through you. Never lose sight of the fact that it's Him who really does the talking. We're just the mouthpieces. Second, some of these seven imperatives took me years to learn, and there are a couple that took longer still.

"I guess what I'm trying to say is that you shouldn't get discouraged if things don't change overnight. This, like most things, is a process. The more you speak and the more you listen to yourself, the more you'll understand. Before long you won't be able to preach any other way."

The two men got out of the truck, made their way through the terminal, and located the gleaming Harlan Enterprises Gulfstream. "There's something I want you to have." Will handed Ray a small, worn notebook.

"What is this, Will?"

"It's a notebook I've kept over the years that contains the seven imperatives we've discussed. Everything we've talked about and a couple of things we haven't is in there. I want you to take it so you won't forget anything."

"I can't," Ray protested. "You've got a lot of preaching ahead of you. You might need it."

"Like I said, Ray, it's all in here." Will patted his heart. "Before long, I'm trusting God that it will be a part of you just like it's a part of me."

Ray smiled, tucking the notebook safely into his coat pocket. "Does that mean I'll be able to drive a big rig someday?"

"Only if you're a lucky man, Ray." Will watched his new friend board the private jet and lifted his hand.

Ray caught the gesture. *A blessing?* If so, he'd take it.

Wow. He smiled as he buckled himself in. *This really is the only way to travel!* As the small craft taxied on the runway, Ray's mind was already at home. It was Tuesday, and Sunday was coming. Those old, cold fingers of dread began to wrap around his heart. Would this Sunday really be any different? He knew that the people of Meadowland Community Church would still be there and that he would need to deliver.

He pulled the little notebook out of his pocket. Thumbing through it, the phrases came back to him: Determine Your Goal, Pick a Point, Create a Map, Internalize the Message, Engage Your Audience, Find Your Voice, and Find Some Traction.

The private jet lifted off as he returned the notebook to his pocket and sank back into the buttery soft leather.

He could do this. God would be there to help him.

As the little jet soared into the evening sky, he felt something stirring down inside him. Something he hadn't experienced in too long a time.

Excitement.

Part

2

COMMUNICATING FOR A
CHANGE

It's too bad that so few of us have a Will Graham in our lives. Imagine how much more effective we would be in our communication if someone were to take the time to listen and evaluate us at that level. That kind of coaching is rare in the field of communication. That's one reason we decided to write this book. Lane and I have been serving as the Willy Grahams in the lives of a handful of communicators for the past eight years. As unrealistic as some of the dialogue between Ray and Will may have seemed, most of it was inspired by actual conversations (and confrontations) we have had in our roles as communication coaches. You will hear several of those stories in the chapters that follow.

The remainder of this book is a detailed explanation of the *seven imperatives*. You may find some of our ideas challenging, perhaps even a bit unorthodox. But before you dismiss these ideas as impractical, let me place them in a context we can all understand. If you saw your three-year old child reaching for a scorpion what wouldn't you do to stop her? I imagine you would be willing to forgo all the rules of normal, even decent, behavior to keep her hand away from that scorpion's sting. You would raise your voice. You would run in the house. You would leap over the furniture. You would risk bodily harm if that's what it took to keep her out of danger. You would do whatever it took.

Every single person who sits politely and listens to you on Sunday is one decision away from moral, financial, and marital ruin. Every one of 'em. Many are considering options with consequences that will follow them the remainder of their lives. There are husbands teetering on the brink of unfaithfulness. Wives whose schedules are unsustainable. Couples who are drowning in a sea of debt. Teenagers who are there because their parents forced them to come. Young men who have been told they are gay. Young ladies who have been told their worth goes no further than their physical beauty.

There they sit. Silent. Waiting. Hoping. Doubting. Anticipating. What are we going to do? What are you going to do? What are you going to say?

This is the world we have been called to address. These are the issues we have been called to confront. There is much at stake. There are many at risk. The great news is the pages of Scripture are filled with principles, narratives, and truth that address each of those needs. The question you must answer is, to what extreme are you willing to go to create a delivery system that will connect with the heart of your audience? Are you willing to abandon a style, an approach, a system that was designed in another era for a culture that no longer exists? Are you willing to step out of your comfort zone in order to step into the lives God has placed in your care? Are you willing to make the adjustment? Will you consider letting go of your alliterations and acrostics and three point outlines and talk to people in terms they understand? Will you communicate for life change?

11

DETERMINE YOUR GOAL

What are you trying to accomplish?

We've all walked to our cars after a message feeling like we knocked it out of the park. And, we've all slithered out the back door, hoping we didn't have to make eye contact with anybody. There have been many Sundays when I felt like I owed the audience an apology for making them endure whatever it was I did up there for forty minutes. That's one advantage of preaching multiple times on a weekend. I usually get at least one out of three right. Usually.

For the most part, our feelings about how we did are tied to our own judgement of our performance; how well we delivered the illustration, handled the text, remembered our transitions, made our point, and landed the plane. That's normal.

But, regardless of what we say, we care more about what others think. And, if you are like me, you care most in the hour following the delivery of a message. It is during that hour that we regain the much needed perspective that comes with realizing who we are and who we aren't. It is during the drive home that we realize we can't change the world with a good sermon. But neither will all of Christendom collapse because of a bad one.

But during and immediately following a message, we are vulnerable. Our egos are on the line. We are self-conscious. Easily wounded. If you've got something good to say to me about my message, bring it on immediately. If you have a "suggestion," wait until Wednesday. Even if I ask for suggestions, wait until Wednesday. In the meantime, lie if you have to. Tell me it was great. If it wasn't, don't worry, I already know.

Preaching is a performance. Preachers are performers. But unlike the comedian, we are expected to do more than entertain. We are expected to be educational, inspirational, theological, and engaging all at the same time. So there we stand. All alone. All eyes on us. Waiting. Expecting. Hoping. And did I mention that we have to talk to the same audience week after week? Did I mention that all week long they have been driving around in their cars listening to my dad, Chuck Swindoll, Ed Young, and Sean Hannity. Whose idea was this?

It is no wonder that our feelings about how we did are tied to our performance. There's a lot of pressure on us to perform. But in spite of that, the scope of our evaluation must reach beyond our presentation. While we must pay attention to and work to improve our performance on the platform, there is something else to consider as well. Namely, *the outcome*. What people do as a result of what we say. The audience's willingness to act on what they have heard. Life change.

As long as our feelings about how we did are tied only to our performance in the moment, then the moment won't count for much. If you think about it, your delivery, your style, your humor, your conclusion, your timing is all about...you guessed it...you. At some point we've got to begin caring more for the people in the audience than the person on the platform. When we do, our presentations take on real significance. Until we do, communication is really all about us.

So before we launch in to a discussion about "How," let's spend a few minutes talking about "What." *What* are you trying to accomplish? *What* is your goal in communicating? *What* is the win? *What* do you want to look back on as a result of your years of preaching and teaching?

This is an extraordinarily important question. Why? Because *our approach to communicating should be shaped by our goal in communicating*. Most of us inherited our approach to communicating. We grew up listening to preachers who all took basically the same approach. Then we went to schools where we were taught to develop messages along the lines of the style we grew up listening to. Chances are, nobody challenged you to think through your goal as a communicator. They just taught you an approach. But if your approach to communicating does not support your goal as a communicator there is a disconnect. You will spend hours preparing messages that are not designed to accomplish what you are passionate about accomplishing.

So, what is your goal? Your goal will determine whether or not you like my approach. Because the approach we are about to discuss is driven by a very specific goal.

THREE POSSIBILITIES

It would not be helpful at this juncture to list all the possible goals for communicating from the Scriptures. It might be helpful, however, to focus on the three that fuel the majority of communicators in our churches. The first one is: *Teach the Bible to people*. The idea here is to teach the content of the Bible so that interested parties can understand and navigate their way through the Scriptures.

This is usually the goal of the preacher or teacher who methodically and systematically teaches verse by verse through books of the Bible. This is the perfect approach for the communicator whose goal is to simply explain what the Bible means. Wherever we left off last week, we will pick it up again next week. This approach requires no creativity. This approach need not include any application. This approach assumes a great deal of interest by the audience. And honestly, this approach is easy when compared to other methods of communication.

I saw this approach taken to an extreme on an Easter Sunday in Dallas, Texas. I visited a Bible church with some friends. On the way they explained that their pastor was preaching through the book of Psalms. They were in their forty-third week. Easter would be week forty-four. And sure enough, on Easter Sunday this guy picked up with Psalm 44. He made a reference to Easter at some point along the way. But it was a stretch. In his defense, he was teaching the Bible to people. And his approach matched his goal.

PEOPLE FIRST

A second possible goal is to *teach people the Bible*. This goal differs from the first in that the communicator takes his audience into account as he plans his approach. After all, the goal is to teach *people*. Communicators who have embraced this goal are constantly looking for effective ways to impart biblical truth into the mind and heart of the hearer. This goal was behind the "three points and an application" approach to preaching. The multipoint sermon or teaching outline is a great approach for the communicator whose goal is to teach people the Bible. Outlining makes it easier for the average listener to follow along.

Preachers and teachers who embrace this goal often use alliteration and multiple illustrations. After all, alliteration and illustrations make it easier for an audience to understand and remember the portions of the text being taught. I worked for a guy once who alliterated the entire book of Jeremiah.

Cool, huh?

Any communication strategy that follows from this second goal requires sensitivity to the audience and therefore some element of creativity. When I was teaching high school students, I developed a rhyme for every chapter in the book of Acts so that they could think their way through the entire book. I'm sure that came in handy on the weekends.

Generally speaking, the primary concern for the communicator whose goal is to teach the Bible to people is: Did I cover the material? The primary concern for the communicator whose goal is to teach people the Bible is: Did my audience understand and will they remember the material? In both cases success is measured in terms of information transfer.

If spiritual maturity were synonymous with information transfer, or more specifically, Bible content transfer, then either of the above options would be fine.

But it's not. And you know that. I know that. Everybody I know knows that. The people that don't know that wouldn't read this book anyway.

You and I know that Bible knowledge can lead to pride; the antithesis of spiritual maturity.[1] It's interesting that the group who knew the Old Testament Scriptures best were the very ones who considered Jesus a blasphemer and arranged for His crucifixion. Knowing isn't enough.

HEARING AND DOING

A third goal, and the one I subscribe to, is to *teach people how to live a life that reflects the values, principles, and truths of the Bible.* In short, my goal is change. I want them to do something different instead of just think about it.

When I'm finished preaching, I want people in the audience to know what to do with what they have heard. And I want them to walk away motivated to give it a try. This goal flows from what I understand the Bible to teach regarding spiritual maturity. The way I read it, spiritual maturity is gauged by application not contemplation. James says it best, "Faith without deeds is useless."[2] "Do not merely listen to the word, and so deceive yourselves. Do what it says."[3]

Jesus weighed in on the subject as well, "By this all men will know that you are my disciples, if you love one another."[4] When asked which of the commandments were the greatest He summarized the entire law with two action-oriented imperatives, love God and love your neighbor.

My friend Randy Pope expressed it this way, "Preaching is not talking to people *about* the Bible; it is talking to people about *themselves* from the Bible."[5]

So here's my point. *Preaching for change requires a different approach to communication than either of the previous two goals we discussed.* Every communicator I know wants to see lives changed as a result of their preaching and teaching. But too few communicators have developed an approach to communicating that supports their passion. They simply adapted the approach handed down to us from a previous generation.

Preaching for life change requires far less information and more application. Less explanation and more inspiration. Less first century and more twenty-first century. While I'm a firm believer that all Scripture is equally inspired, observation tells me that all Scripture is not equally applicable. Consequently, preaching for life change requires that we emphasize some texts over others.

Now before you close this book and write me off as a heretic, consider this. If a preacher spends a year teaching verse by verse through the book of John, would you accuse him of neglecting the other sixty-five books? I don't think so. In fact, you may applaud him for being thorough. My point is, we all pick and choose. None of us give equal time to every passage of Scripture.

Preaching for life change involves picking those passages that are most appropriate for and applicable to our target audience. This is what Jesus did. This is what the apostle Paul did. They addressed felt needs and supported their teaching with references from the Old Testament. Nowhere in the Scriptures is there an example of, or reference to, anyone teaching through a book of the Old Testament. They knew better.

I find it particularly amusing when I hear of pastors spending months preaching through one of the epistles. Think about it. Each epistle is a carefully written argument addressing the specific issues of a specific church. So what do we do? We carefully exegete a letter written to a first-century church about the issues they were facing while ignoring what's happening right in front of us. If we really want to take our cue from the apostle Paul we should address the specific issues confronting the people in our audience. That's why I weave a message about sexual purity or money into just about every series we do. It's why we program an entire series around family life every spring. Those are three issues that consume the time and attention of the average man and woman. Fortunately for us, the Scripture has a lot to say about all three.

When you commit to preach for life change, your preparation is not complete until you have answered two very important questions: So what? and Now what?[6] Our preaching won't make much difference if our people don't understand what difference it is supposed to make. Our audience won't do much with what we've taught until we tell 'em what they ought to do.

With the first goal we discussed the teacher feels successful if he covers the material. A preacher or teacher who embraces the second goal feels successful if the audience is engaged. But if you decide to preach for life change you won't be satisfied until the behavior of your audience is transformed; and you will be willing to do just about anything to see that transpire.

At the end of the day, I want the people in my congregation to trust God with every arena of their lives: family, finances, career, relationships, everything. That kind of trust is developed when we act on what we know. Acts of obedience allow our faith to intersect with God's faithfulness. It is at that intersection that we see God work. And when we see Him work our faith gets bigger.

WHEN ALL IS SAID AND DONE

So what's your goal? How do you define success? Which concerns you more, how you *did* on Sunday or what your people are *doing* on Monday? And if it is the latter, *does your approach to communicating support what you are trying to accomplish?* Or does it compete?

You may not embrace my approach. That's fine. But I pray you will embrace this goal. We have enough hearers. The church in America in particular has been listening for generations. We need doers, appliers. That means we need sermons that are loaded with application and preaching that is communicated with inspiration. Will you make it your goal to lead your people to do and not just hear? And would you commit to doing whatever you have to do to bring them to that point, regardless of the changes it requires of you?

Several years ago I was talking to one of our communicators right before he was about to go out and deliver his message. I could tell by his body language that he was trying desperately to keep everything straight in his head. He so badly wanted to get it right, to do a good job. That's always a red flag for me. He was about to walk out and do what we've all done so many times. He was about to step on the platform consumed with how well he would perform. So I called him over to the side and gave him a version of the same talk I give myself when I sense that I've become so concerned with my content that I've forgotten my audience. I said...

"How would you communicate this message if your eighteen-year-old son had made up his mind to walk away from everything you have taught him, morally, ethically, and theologically, unless he had a compelling reason not to? What would you say this morning if you knew that was at stake? Because for somebody's son out there this may be his last chance. Now quit worrying about your outline. Go out there and plead your case like your own son's future was at stake."

And he did.

So what's your goal? What are you after when you speak or teach? What is the win? Smarter people? Changed people? People with more confidence in God? This is a very important question. Because your approach to communicating needs to match your goal. If at the end of the day the win for you is stories of life-change, then perhaps we can help you develop an approach that fits your goal. If you are satisfied with simply teaching the Bible to people or even communicating to people about the Bible, I'm not sure you have the right book. But now that you've gotten this far, you might as well keep reading.

TAKEAWAY

- Our approach to communicating should be shaped by our goal in communicating.

- Our goal should be life change. Specifically, to teach people how to live a life that reflects the values, principles, and truths of the Bible.

- When you commit to preach for life change, your preparation is not complete until you have answered two very important questions: So what? and Now what?[6]

12

PICK A POINT

What are you trying to say?

If you compare public speaking to taking people on a journey, then it follows that the communicator should *attempt* to pick everyone up at the same station and deliver them to the same destination. The approach we are developing throughout this book assumes that the communicator has a destination in mind; a single idea they want to communicate; a specific thing he or she hopes to accomplish. And once that point, that idea, that destination is clear, then the goal is to bend everything in the message towards that one thing.

Every journey begins and ends somewhere. The same can be said for every talk. A good journey is planned with the end in mind. The same *should* be said of every sermon. Unfortunately, what most of us grew up hearing were messages built around several points rather than one clear destination. To make things worse, many of us were actually trained in that model. You know what I'm talking about…

"God wants a man to…

I. Love his wife

II. Lead his wife

III. Learn from his wife

...*but never ever*...

IV. Leave his wife

A problem with this approach is that by the time you get to your last point, nobody remembers the first three. Whatever impact they might have made is washed away by the information and illustrations that follow. On a good day, it is that last point that usually sticks. And that's assuming it was stated in a way that made it memorable.

The other problem with preaching points is that it doesn't reflect the world we live in. We don't live our lives by points. We live by our emotions. We respond to what we see, taste, and feel. So there's no compelling reason to remember a list of points. They never come in handy. For anything. Even the preacher giving the points knows this. That's why he or she has to refer to their notes. They haven't even bothered to memorize their own points. How ironic. Our points flow from our notes to the listener's notebooks, assuming they bothered to bring them. In most cases, our *allusive, alluring, alliterated* points move from our notes to our lips into thin air and then back into our files. Seems a bit pointless.

The point of points is to move people systematically through an outline. And if that's your goal, stick with your points. Good things will come of it. But if life change is your goal, point by point preaching is not the most effective approach.

Now if you are a point by point preacher you may and possibly should take offense at that last statement. The implication is that your point by point preaching has not resulted in life change. And chances are you can point to people in your congregation whose lives have been greatly impacted by your preaching. So who am I to dis your entire approach when there is evidence to the contrary?

Let me say it again, If life change is your *goal*, point by point preaching is not the *most* effective approach. All I'm arguing is that there is a better approach, not that point by point preaching is completely ineffective. I grew up in the world of point by point preaching. My dad is the king of points. And through the years hundreds of thousands of people would readily admit that their lives have been changed through his preaching. But here is my observation. It is not the points that resulted in life change. It was the passion and the specific call to action with which he ends his messages that move people to live differently and surrender more fully. And I bet the same is true of your preaching. Let's face it, of your three or four points from last week's message, I bet you chose the most powerful one to end with; the one that inspired people to change. In the pages that follow I want to teach you how to build your entire message around a single point.

WHAT'S THE POINT?

When I say *point* I am referring to one of three things: an application, an insight, or a principle. With this approach, every message should have one central idea, application, insight, or principle that serves as the glue to hold the other parts together. On a more macro level, every message series should as well.

Perhaps an illustration would help. I just completed a series on the three temptations of Jesus entitled *Pause*. The point of the series is: *Temptation is always a test of your faith, not just your self-control.* We came back to that idea throughout the series. But each message within the series was designed to make one specific point as well. They are as follows:

- Temptation can steal your future, your family, and your faith.
- Pause before you seek to meet physical needs in irresponsible ways.
- Cooperate with God, don't attempt to manipulate Him.
- Never trade the immediate for the important.

The big idea for the series, as well as my point for the first message in the series, is an insight. The points for the second two messages are imperatives or applications. Again, the point we are looking for takes one of several forms, but there's always a point, a destination, a bottom line.

TWO THINGS

The key to this approach is refusing to stand up and speak until you know the answer to two questions:

- What is the one thing I want my audience to know?
- What do I want them to do about it?

Those are two frustrating questions. I have pushed back from my computer on many occasions thinking I'm finished with my prep, when it occurs to me I have three pages of outline but I don't have an answer for those two questions.

"But wait," you argue, "What if there are two things I want them to know?" That's great, now you have a two-part series. Seriously, pick one and focus on it.

But let's face it, the average communicator isn't even trying to narrow his talk to two things. The feedback I generally get is more along the lines of, "But what if there are *several* things I want them to know?" Save it.

There are plenty of Sundays to go around. No doubt you have sat through messages that could have been an entire series. The outline I laid out at the beginning of this chapter is a good example of that. One of my favorite communicators told me that on several occasions his wife has turned to him after a message and said, "I really enjoyed the *sermons*."

With this approach you pick one idea, principle, application, or insight and build around it. In any one sermon you are going to say a dozen or more helpful, potentially life changing things. And we've all had people tell us how much something we said meant to them and we don't remember saying it. We can't control how and where information lands with our audience. Their life experience forms a grid through which they filter everything they hear. All I'm suggesting is that instead of choosing two or three or four ideas to leave with your audience, just pick one.

THE DISCOVERY

In the following paragraphs I'm going to lay out everything I know about finding, developing, and building around a single point. But if you have been preaching or teaching for any length of time, my hunch is that your challenge will not be *finding* the one, but *eliminating* the three. By the time you have finished preparing your message, you pretty much know where the force of the message is; you know where the "a-ha" moment is. By the time you've finished preparing, you know the part of your message that excites you the most. In other words, you know *how* to find the main point. You know *when* you've found the main point. What you need to focus on is building everything around it.

If your reaction to that idea is, "But sometimes I don't know what *it* is until late in the preparation game," then you are on the right track.

I almost never know what it is until very late in the game. And when I finally hit it, or it hits me, I have to go back and clear away all the clutter so that it is *the* point rather than *a* point. I reorganize to it, rather than letting it sit in the outline with a lot of extra stuff around it. There have been many a Saturday night when I've walked into the kitchen and said to Sandra, "I have no point. Four pages of outline and no point!" Fortunately that's the exception, not the rule.

The process of developing a one point message can be broken down as follows:

1. Dig until you find it.
2. Build everything around it.
3. Make it stick.

Chapter thirteen focuses on the second step, so I'll only touch on it briefly here.

1. Dig until you find it.

The reason the *one thing* usually comes late in the game is that sermon preparation is a discovery process. Preparation involves discovering what the text says and what it doesn't say, what we wish it would say, what we didn't expect it to say. At the same time message preparation involves holding up the text to the scrutiny of experience. Bridging the cultural divide of first and twenty-first century isn't always easy…but it is always necessary if we are going to communicate for change rather than information transfer.

If our goal is to teach people how to live a life that reflects the values and principles of Scripture, then the one thing should ultimately find its source in the text. But it is possible to develop an entire sermon outline that accurately reflects what a text is teaching and yet still not have one strong unifying idea. I'm afraid too many preachers are content to simply "preach the Word" without taking the time to distill the one thing that needs to be highlighted from the "Word." More on that in a minute.

On rare occasions I know the point before I begin my official preparation. Sometimes it emerges from life rather than from the text. Sometimes I bump into an idea, principle, or application in the course of life and then go looking for biblical support. That approach was highly discouraged in seminary. And understandably so. Obviously we've got to be careful not to try and force the Scripture to support our ideas and observations. But you never know when and where you might come across something true and helpful. Often someone will share an insight or idea in my home group that serves as an organizing idea for a message. I imagine you've experienced the same thing. Because insight can originate from the text or from life we must be students of both.

When I bump into an idea that I think might serve as the driving force for a message or series, here are the types of questions I ask:

- What, if anything, does the Bible say about this?
- If nothing, why?
- Who, in the Scriptures, faced a situation that forced them to interface with this topic or idea?
- What did they do? What didn't they do that I might have expected them to do?
- Did Jesus ever address this topic directly or indirectly?

At that point I try to take my hands off the wheel and let the text direct me instead of the other way around. Once you discover a text or narrative that addresses your *great idea*, let the Bible speak. Even if the text contradicts your idea or assumptions going in, let the text speak. It is in that tension that you will make some of your greatest discoveries.

When our minds are made up going in, we unintentionally resist the influence of the Holy Spirit. That's when we run the risk of misusing the text.

The toughest sermon I have ever preached was on the topic of divorce and remarriage. I don't like what Jesus said about remarriage. On the surface it seems to condemn the victim as well as limit their options going forward. It was tempting to skip what He said and dive right into the apostle Paul's more user-friendly approach. But I decided instead to limit the message to what Jesus said on the subject.[7] No hedging. No trying to make it fit with other parts of the New Testament. The *point* for that message was: *You can't un-one what God has made one.*

Popular notion.

I told our folks how uncomfortable I was with the whole subject and especially Jesus' ideas. But, what He said, He said for a reason. As I closed in on my one point, I took two glass pitchers of water, one with red food coloring, the other with green, and poured them together into an empty glass container. The text as well as the illustration made the one point unmistakably and in some cases painfully clear. You could have heard a pin drop.

When you make an uncomfortable discovery in the text (and there are plenty) the best question to ask is, "Why would a God who claims to love us and demonstrated His love say such a thing?" Whenever I take the time and make the effort to wrestle that question to the ground I always learn something new. As it turned out, that message turned out to be a tremendous encouragement for divorced and remarried couples. How? Because any time we help people discover where they are and where they aren't they have a clearer understanding of how to get where they need to go.

My point? Let the text speak for itself. When it agrees with your preconceived ideas, great. When it doesn't, dig in and learn something. And keep digging until you unearth the one thing.

We do an event every quarter called "Married Life Live." The purpose of this event is to focus our married couples on *one* of six marriage essentials. These six essentials are what we believe to be the irreducible minimums for a good marriage. We focus on one each quarter until we cover all six, then start over. But when we start over we change the presentation. So over the course of several years couples will hear several different presentations on each of the essentials.

One of those essentials is "Nurture Romance." A couple of years ago our married life director asked Lane Jones, the coauthor of this book, to do the keynote on that particular essential at our Married Life event. Obviously there is a lot that can be said about nurturing romance in a marriage. But Lane was committed to picking a point.

By committing to build his talk around one thing rather than a list of things that nurture romance, Lane stumbled upon a simple yet profound insight that served as the big idea for the night. His entire talk centered around this one idea: *You are the only legitimate source of romance in your spouse's life.* Instead of focusing our attention on how to get something from our spouse, he focused our attention on our unique roll. Again, simple but profound. Where did that idea come from? A combination of Bible study, discussion, observation, and an overarching commitment to dig until he found *the* insight around which to build his message. Once you commit to this approach and determine not to quit digging until you find *the* point, you will be amazed at what you unearth. In Lane's case it would have been much easier to give our folks a list of things. But lists go on paper. Single, powerful ideas have a way of penetrating the heart.

2. Build everything around it.

As I mentioned earlier, once you discover the *one thing*, the next step is to go back and orient your entire message around your point. Remember, we are taking people on a journey. Once you've identified the destination, you owe it to your audience to make the path clear and direct. That means you cut away the things that are not pertinent to the subject. You know what I'm talking about. The filler. The stuff you've thrown in because you are concerned about having enough to say. Sure, you need some of that in the initial preparation stages. That story you love to tell. That one liner that always gets a laugh. That insight that you are sure is original with you. That nuance in the original language that will impress people with your scholarship. But once you unearth that singular idea, insight, or application the filler has got to go. Ask yourself, *Does this really facilitate the journey or is this just something that will get a laugh or fill time?*

This can be a frustrating process. If you have spent three or four hours dissecting four or five juicy nuggets from a text, you feel like you need to share 'em all! What a waste to leave so much good stuff on the cutting room floor. But that's exactly what you must discipline yourself to do. Cutting away the peripheral is like narrowing a channel of water. You end up with a much more focused and powerful message people are able to follow, tracking with you as you lead them along. And all that extra stuff? Save it. Sunday comes around every week.

I meet with all our staff communicators two or three times before they deliver a message on Sunday morning. The most painful part of our meeting is when I look at them and say, "Here's your main idea, now go back and rearrange everything around it." It is painful because that entails cutting out some really good stuff. And besides, they thought they were finished. If you don't take the time to reorient your message around the one thing, it will get lost amongst the other things.

More on that in the next chapter.

3. Make it stick.

Once you have discovered your point and rebuilt your message around it, the next step is to craft a single statement or phrase that makes it stick. It needs to be as memorable as possible. This will help you as well as your audience. If it is short and memorable then it will be easier for you to blend it in throughout your message. If it is a well-crafted statement, it will be more obvious to your audience that this is your point.

Generally speaking, people will not be impacted by a paragraph. Nobody remembers a paragraph. People are impacted by statements that stick. You need a sticky statement. Take the time to reduce your one point to one sticky statement. It doesn't need to be cute. It doesn't have to rhyme. But it should be short and memorable. Your statement is your anchor. It is what holds the message together and keeps it from drifting off course. This will be what people remember.

Here are some examples

- Your friends determine the direction and quality of your life
- Purity paves the way to intimacy
- When you see as God sees, you will do as God says
- Submission is an invitation to lead
- Everybody lives forever somewhere
- Acceptance fuels influence
- Good people don't go to heaven, forgiven people do
- God takes full responsibility for the life fully devoted to Him
- Cooperate don't manipulate
- To understand why, submit and apply
- Others first
- Maximum freedom is found under God's authority

Your point can be a statement taken right out of the Scriptures. When I talk to students about their friends the *one thing* is the first half of Proverbs 13:20, "He who walks with the wise grows wise." I developed a message on purity from 1 Corinthians 6:18. My point was one word, "Flee!"

On occasions the one point has been a question. We did a series on the life of Joseph. The question I asked throughout was, "What would somebody who is you do if they were absolutely confident that God was with them?" I just kept coming back to that question throughout the narrative.

When preaching through John 6, my point was a question from the text, "To whom shall we go?"[8] I'll never forget a letter I received about a year later from a college freshman. She was in her dorm the first week of her first semester and everybody was going crazy. She said she sat there wondering if she should put Christianity on hold for a while and join the fun. She wrote, "As I was sitting there your question popped into my head, 'To whom shall I go? To whom shall I go? If not Christ, who?'" That night she reaffirmed her decision to follow Christ in college. By the end of her freshman year she had established herself as a leader in her sorority. She started a Bible study. During her undergraduate studies she led several of her sisters to faith. She points to that night as a defining moment. Those weren't my words. But she heard that question asked so many times throughout that message that it stuck in her heart. And the Holy Spirit surfaced it at a critical time.

Creating a statement that sticks is a step most communicators skip. I understand why. By the time I get to this point in the preparation process I'm tired. Surely after thirty or forty minutes of hearing me talk people are smart enough to know what I'm saying. Possibly. But as soon as they head for their cars it starts slipping away. It is not enough to say it. We need to say it in a way that makes it stick. Unless…unless your goal is just information transfer. If you are simply teaching the Bible or even teaching people the Bible, a well-crafted, memorable statement is not necessary. Just cover your material and leave it at that.

I am convinced that this one extra step makes all the difference. But again, I know why most communicators don't do it. You don't need it to keep people awake or engaged. But if you are concerned about what happens once they leave the room, you better make it stick.

BURDEN BEARER

Thus far our discussion has been somewhat academic. Get a point. Make it memorable. Yawn. But there is another aspect to one point preaching and teaching that is anything but academic. In fact, it is this dimension of the one point message that drives me to keep searching for the one thing among the many. My dad has a word for it. He calls it the preacher's "burden."

My dad and I have a standing breakfast appointment on the first Thursday of every month. It is something I always look forward to. Eventually the discussion always makes its way around to church stuff. On this particular morning we got on the subject of preaching. Now If you have heard my dad preach, you know he is the master of points. Why have three when you can have eight? Or twelve? He's been preaching that way for years. Note takers love him. Actually, a lot of people love him. Anyway, I was going on and on about this idea of building the message around one point when he interrupted me with, "You've got to have a burden. That's the thing most preachers are missing. A burden. If they don't have a burden it's just a bunch of fluff."

As we continued our conversation, it became apparent that when he talked about a preacher's burden he was referring to the *one thing*. That one message, idea, principle, or truth that had to be delivered at all cost. The one thing isn't just information. It is not just a carefully crafted phrase. It is literally a burden. It is a burden that weighs so heavily on the heart of the communicator that he or she must deliver it. And he was right, you can tell when a communicator is carrying a burden versus when he is simply dispensing information.

At some point in the preparation process, you must stop and ask yourself, "What is the one thing I must communicate? What is it that people have to know?" If you don't have an answer to that question, you aren't ready. Think about it. If after all your preparation you can't answer that question, what's the point in preaching? If YOU don't know what it is you are dying to communicate, the audience certainly isn't going to be able to figure it out.

Is there anything you are so excited about sharing that you can't wait until you get to that part of the message? If not, you aren't ready. You don't have a burden. You may have pages of information and it may all be true, but if you don't have something that people need so badly that you feel compelled to share it, you still have work to do.

The sermons that have put you to sleep were delivered by men with information but no burden. A burden brings passion to preaching. It transforms lifeless theology into compelling truth. When I talk to high school students about purity, my message is simple: Purity paves the way to intimacy. But it is more than a principle. It is more than a cute phrase. It is a burden I carry for teenagers. It is something they've got to know.

Reducing your message to one idea will allow you to create an entire talk around the one thing you most want to communicate. It makes memorizing, embracing, or owning the message so much easier. Why? Because your goal is to deliver that one point. As long as you're making sense and moving in the direction toward the intended destination, then it doesn't really matter what you leave out along the way. What matters is that you're bringing the audience along with you.

BUT WHAT ABOUT...

On occasion someone will ask, "But isn't it the job of the Holy Spirit to take the Scripture and work it into the heart's and minds of the listener as he sees fit? If so, who are we to limit the work of the Spirit by limiting the scope of the message to one thing?"

I agree, it is the job of the Holy Spirit to take the spoken word and convict, convince, and change the hearer. And we have no control over which part of what we say the Spirit might choose to use. Further, I think you would agree that the Holy Spirit often takes different ideas, illustrations, and insights from the same message and applies them to different people in various ways. After all, He's like the wind. You can't harness Him. He will do as He pleases.

But if we are going to let that truth shape our preparation, why organize a message at all? Why not just get up and start talking, sprinkle in a few verses and trust the Holy Spirit to do His thing? Actually, I've heard guys speak that left me with the impression that that's exactly what they were doing. It was interesting, but not all that helpful.

If you are going to use any kind of organizational structure at all, albeit one point, three points, four points, storytelling, or testimony, you have already made a decision to limit the scope of what you are planning to say. Face it, once you pick a text (or two) you have limited the scope of the message. All I'm saying is pick one and stay with it.

Besides, it is easier for people to follow a message built around a single idea. Easy to follow translates into enjoyable to experience. And if they enjoy the communication experience they are likely to come back for more. And if they keep coming back for more they are going to be exposed to more truth which gives the Holy Spirit more opportunities to speak to them. So you could argue that a one point message is *more* conducive to the work of the Spirit.

Let's face it, the reason so many churches are half full on Sunday morning is because a whole bunch of people decided not to come back. Why? The preacher didn't give 'em anything to come back for. There were plenty of points, but nothing worth coming back for the following week.

In the next chapter I'm going to introduce a new kind of outlining technique that is designed to keep a single point in view throughout a message. But honestly, the next chapter isn't going to do you much good unless you are willing to *pick a point*. I know that for many this runs against the grain of everything you've been taught and seen modeled. I know it leaves you wondering, "But what am I going to talk about for twenty or thirty minutes?" But I also know that if you will try it, if you will make up your mind once and for all that your goal is not to fill up your allotted time, but to communicate for life change, then this approach may liberate you as a communicator. Now go pick a point.

TAKEAWAY

- In a one point message it is essential for the communicator to know the answer to two questions: What is the one thing I want my audience to know? What do I want them to do about it?

- For most communicators the biggest challenge will not be finding the *one* idea, but eliminating the other three.

- The process for developing a one point message is as follows:

  1. Dig until you find it

  2. Build everything around it

  3. Make it stick.

13

CREATE A MAP

What's the best route to your point?

Once you pick a point, you need a way to introduce it, support it, and apply it to your audience. So now comes the tedious work of developing an outline. If you have been communicating for any length of time I'm sure you have a style or format that works for you. I have friends who manuscript. I know a guy who mind-maps. One well respected communicator that we all know confided in me that he prepares everything in his head. No written outline. To each his own.

Now while it is true that there is no one "right" way to outline a message, I have discovered a method that has proven to be extraordinarily effective for organizing material around a single point. This outlining method is built around the communicator's relationship with the audience rather than content. After all, the way we organize material on paper is very different from how we process information in a conversation. (Try outlining a conversation with your spouse.) For that reason, this method allows the message to retain a conversational quality.

The outline revolves around five words, each of which represents a section of the message. They are:

ME, WE, GOD, YOU, WE.

With this approach the communicator introduces a dilemma he or she has faced or is currently facing (ME). From there you find common ground with your audience around the same or a similar dilemma (WE). Then you transition to the text to discover what God says about the tension or question you have introduced (GOD). Then you challenge your audience to act on what they have just heard (YOU). And finally, you close with several statements about what could happen in your community, your church, or the world, if everybody embraced that particular truth (WE).

Each of the five components plays a specific and important role in facilitating the communication journey. ME orients the audience to the topic. It answers the question, "What is he/she talking about?" WE assures the audience that this is a relevant topic for them. It allows the communicator to identify with the audience. The GOD section serves as illumination. Here is where we bring a new perspective to or shine fresh light on a specific tension. YOU is simply application. WE is the placeholder for inspiration.

ME	WE	GOD	YOU	WE
Orientation	Identification	Illumination	Application	Inspiration

Perhaps an example would help. Let's assume your topic is marriage. There are dozens of things you could say about marriage, but you have narrowed it down to one thing: *Submission is the best decision.* The idea being that our first response should be to put the needs and desires of our spouse ahead of our own. With that in mind, here's how the MWGYW outline might look.

INTRODUCTION:

ME—Sometimes I find myself wondering how to respond to situations in my marriage.

WE—I imagine you have found yourself in situations where you weren't sure what to do either.

GOD—The Bible teaches that we are to submit to one another; put the desires and needs of our spouse ahead of our own needs and desires.

YOU—Next time you aren't sure what to say or do, ask yourself this question, "How can I put the needs and desires of my spouse ahead of my own in this moment?"

Conclusion: In a marriage, submission is generally the best decision.

WE—Imagine what would happen in our community if all of us began to model that kind of mutual submission before our friends and neighbors.

ME

By starting with a statement or story about myself I am able to introduce myself as well as the topic to the audience. This is especially important when addressing a new audience. But ME isn't really about me. ME is about finding common ground with THEM. Common ground is an essential to any relationship. Especially a communicator's relationship with an audience. An audience has to buy into the messenger before they buy into the message. You know from your own experience that if there is something that bugs you about the communicator it's difficult to engage with their content. This is especially true if they don't seem genuine. A lack of genuineness makes it difficult to trust a speaker. You may even catch yourself resisting and arguing with their content.

Now, what is easy to spot from the audience is difficult to see from the stage. Nobody is arrogant or insincere or slick on purpose. But it happens all the time. And in most cases the communicator never knows it is happening. Five minutes into a talk and she has lost her audience. And doesn't have a clue. Or if they do sense something is wrong, they don't know why.

Recently I received some very negative feedback from a talk I gave at a Youth Specialties Conference. I was really surprised by the reaction. The talk I had given was one I had done on many occasions and had received overwhelmingly positive feedback. So I was shocked to hear that "hundreds of student leaders walked out in the middle." Some actually booed me.

Intrigued, I contacted my host at the conference and asked for a copy of the talk. He graciously sent me one, along with his comments. He assured me that on most occasions he really enjoyed my leadership messages, but this particular one was not one of his favorites. And he went on from there to tell me why. Again, I was really surprised. I knew what I had said. And again, it wasn't anything I hadn't said before.

But as soon as I started listening to the CD, I knew what had happened. I assumed a relationship with this audience that I did not have. Specifically, at the beginning of my talk my microphone went out. So for the first few minutes I was trying to get the mike to work while a guy from backstage fiddled with my belt pack. A bit unnerving in front of five thousand student pastors. I am very committed to staying within the allotted time given. Especially in an environment that is programming heavy. So as they continued to mess with my microphone I was watching precious time slipping away. The sound gurus decided the headset wasn't going to work so they handed me a handheld mike. By this time I was pretty distracted. So much so that I made a huge communication blunder. Actually two. First, I skipped my introductory remarks and went right to the notes. Big mistake.

In my introduction I was planning to talk about the tensions I faced as a student pastor working in a church that was not student friendly. That was my connection with the audience. That was about my only connection with that audience. I'm forty-eight, most of the men and women in attendance were in their late twenties. I skipped ME and consequently it was difficult to convince them that there was much WE. Without meaning to, I positioned myself as a highly opinionated speaker who had little or no empathy for what the average student pastor was dealing with back at home.

The second mistake I made was that I rushed through the material. When a communicator rushes through material it sends a very specific message: I am more concerned about covering my material than I am about communicating with my audience. The emotional message it sends is, I am more concerned about ME than YOU. In my case, when I rush I have a tendency to overcommunicate my point. I can come across very dogmatic. After listening to the message I understood the response. The negative feedback I received focused on my content. But I'm confident the problem was my lack of connection with the audience combined with the tone of my communication.

It is difficult to receive challenging information from someone who seems to have no clue as to what it is like to be you. That is why the ME component of any talk is so important. When handled correctly, an audience finds themselves shaking their heads in agreement and thinking, "Me too." Or in southern vernacular, "You got 'dat right."

How you handle ME will be somewhat determined by your audience. Whenever you're speaking to a new audience, it's critical that you begin with something about yourself, because they don't know you. However, if you're talking to a group that hears you on a regular basis, ME is not as critical. They already know you.

Having said that, I always look for an opportunity to insert my personal struggles with the topic of the day at the front end of a message. After all, on any given Sunday, there will be people in the audience who don't know who I am. And by nature of the fact that I am a preacher, there will be people in the audience trying hard not to like me. Why? Because if they can build a solid case against me as a person, they have an ironclad excuse for ignoring everything I say. So I go out of my way to lay my humanity and frailty out on the front of the stage. Doing so tears down walls. Besides, if you preach from your weakness, you will never run out of material.

WE

Having made it clear to our audience that we are wrestling with a particular tension, the next step is to broaden our tension so as to include everybody listening.

- Sometimes I wonder why I even bother praying (ME). I bet you've wondered about that as well (WE).
- Sometimes I wonder why I am overcome by the same temptations over and over (ME). But that's probably something that only I wrestle with. Right? (WE)
- There are just some people I don't get along with (ME), can anybody here relate to that (WE)?

In this section you need to spend some time applying the tension to as many areas as you can so as to spark an emotion in as broad an audience as possible.

For example, one Christmas I addressed the issue of unmet expectations that seem to be bigger than life during the holiday season. I talked briefly about my family situation and my frustration of not being able to be with both of my parents at Christmas. That was ME. Then I spent a few minutes poking around in just about every family dynamic imaginable, hoping to spark an emotion in as many people as possible.

I addressed the blended family, the single who only has a few days off, the teenager who has to split the holidays with two sets of parents, the prodigal who probably wouldn't show up at all, the loved ones who went to be with the Lord since last Christmas. My goal was to surface the issue of unmet or unmeetable expectations at Christmas. I struggle with it. You struggle with it, too.

Now, if you are reading this book with a highlighter in your hand, I would encourage you to highlight this next sentence. Don't transition from WE to the next section until you feel like you have created a tension that your audience is dying for you to resolve. In other words, assume no interest. Focus on the question you are intending to answer until you are confident your audience wants it answered. Otherwise you are about to spend twenty or thirty minutes of your life answering a question nobody is asking. I imagine you have better things to do.

You've probably heard or read differing opinions on how much of a message should be allotted to application. If you've ever heard Chuck Swindoll, Bruce Wilkinson, or Rick Warren speak to this issue, they all make the case that seventy to eighty percent of the Gospels and Epistles are application oriented. I agree. (I bet those guys will be relieved to know that.)

One of the advantages to this approach is that it wraps the entire message in application. Unlike some methods where the application is tacked on to the end, this approach allows the communicator to introduce a topic within the context of application. If you can get your audience to question something, say "Yeah, me to" about something, or simply wonder, "What *should* I do about that?" you have already crossed over into the realm of application. Application isn't a section of the message, it is the context of the message. The ME-WE-GOD-YOU-WE approach sets you up to address the issue of application in the beginning as well as at the end. If you open the message with *your* struggle (ME), and relate it to *their* struggle (WE), you're already in the arena of applied truth.

But enough about us.

GOD

Now for the meat. The Bible part. The God part. The text! The goal here is to resolve the tension, or at least some of it, by pointing people to God's thoughts on the subject at hand. One of my well-worn transitions goes something like this:

"Well, the good news is, we are not the first people to struggle with this. The people in Jesus' day did as well. Turn with me to… "

Similarly…

"The good news is that we are not the first group to have doubts about God's goodness, King David did as well. Turn with me to…"

Or…

"God must have known we would struggle with this because Jesus addressed this very issue one afternoon on His way to…"

You get the point.

When it comes to handling the text, communicators tend to move towards two extremes at this point. They either skip along the surface of a few verses without really explaining or engaging the text. Or they go down so deep and stay there so long everybody in the audience is gasping for air. The first extreme leaves the audience biblically illiterate. The second extreme reinforces the audience's assumption that they could never understand the Bible on their own.

On one hand you don't want to skimp on the Scripture. On the other hand, you don't want to bog down in the text. This is where sermons lose momentum and get boring. I think it is the fear of losing the audience that motivates so many young preachers to be Scripture light and story heavy. But there is a third option: *Engage the audience with the text.* Don't just read it. Don't explain it to death. *Engage* the audience with it. Take them with you. Make this part of the journey. Make it so fascinating that they are actually tempted to go home and read it on their own. This isn't easy, but it is worth the effort. And how you do this will be somewhat personality driven. In chapter fifteen I'll give you my rules for the road when it comes to keeping an audience engaged with the text.

YOU

As I mentioned earlier, this section is typically referred to as the application of the message. This is where we tell people what to do with what they have heard. This is where we answer the questions "So what?" and "Now what?"

My preference is to find one point of application that I can challenge everybody to embrace. I rarely ask people to make a life-altering commitment to anything. I don't think that is realistic. But I often challenge people to try something for a week, or even a day. Occasionally, I'll ask people to commit to something for a month.

As we are about to discover, finding one application that everybody can get on line with sets you up for the WE aspect of your message. But more importantly, it allows you to stay focused and concise in your communication.

When it seems necessary to broaden the application I find it helpful to think through the concentric circles of relationships. You were probably taught this somewhere along the way.

- How does this apply to me?
- How does this apply to my family relationships?
- How does this apply to my relationships in the community of faith?
- How does this apply to my relationships with those outside the faith?
- How does this apply in the marketplace?

Another way to mine for application is to think through the various stages of life:

- How does this apply to teenagers and college students?
- How does this apply to singles?
- How does this apply to newlyweds?
- How does this apply to parents?
- How does this apply to empty nesters?

I'm not recommending that you walk through all these categories in your message. But by taking the time to think through each of these on your own you will surface some angles that you might have otherwise missed.

There is a third list to think about as well: Believers and unbelievers.

I often address unbelievers at this point in the message. If there is an application for them, I make it. After all, a principle is a principle. Many biblical principles work for anybody. Unconditional love makes an impact regardless of your theology. So does honesty and a dozen other biblical virtues. If I can get an unbeliever to apply a biblical principle and he or she sees results, that's progress.

When a message does not apply to an unbeliever, I let 'em know that as well. In fact I usually let 'em know up front. I often say something to the effect of, "If you are not a believer, you are off the hook today. Just sit back and relax. You are in a guilt-free zone. In fact, today's message may give you another reason to put off becoming a Christian."

The last category I might apply a message to is the person who is not there. Every time you speak, somebody is sitting there thinking about someone who really needed to hear what you had to say. Go ahead and address the person who *is* there but who knows somebody who should have been there. Suggest ways for them to get your message in front of that person, tactfully.

WE

Like you, I love to wrap up a message with an emotionally charged story that punctuates the main point in a way that leaves the audience gasping for breath and reaching for their Kleenex. And every once in a while God graces us with those closing illustrations. But for the other fifty-one weeks of the year we need something else. That's where WE comes in.

This final component of the message is an opportunity for you to rejoin your audience as you did in the beginning of the message when you circled up around your shared frailty, questions, misgivings or temptations. WE is really about vision casting. It is a moment of inspiration. It is the point in the message when you paint a verbal picture of what could be and should be. In this closing moment you call upon your audience to imagine what the church, the community, families, maybe even the world would be like if Christians everywhere embraced your one idea.

Imagine a church where "love one another" was the theme rather than a memory verse for children. Imagine a community dotted with homes where husbands really loved their wives like Christ loved the church. Imagine what would happen in culture if thousands of teenagers abandoned the lie that purity was optional and basically irrelevant. Imagine what could happen in one week if everybody here treated everybody they came into contact with like someone for whom Christ died. Imagine what would happen if for three months we all managed our money as if everything really belongs to God.

This is where you come out from behind whatever it is you preach from and stand off to the side of the stage, as close as you can get to the lip of the stage and dream out loud. Dream on behalf of your church families, singles, kids, churches, the kingdom. This is when you remind your audience that the Scriptures were given not just as a means of making our individual lives better. They were given so that as a body, corporately, we could shine like a beacon of hope in our communities, our neighborhoods, and in the marketplace.

Imagine what WE could do together.

GETTING STARTED

Okay, that's it. But that's a lot. And I imagine that is very different from the way you are currently outlining, so let me close with a couple of suggestions.

Take your last message, or even one you are working on now, and write these five words in the margin where they apply in your current way of outlining. For example, if you typically start your messages by diving right into the text, write GOD out to the side of that section or sections. Write YOU out beside your application. When you are finished, take a shot at rearranging your material around this approach. Use your current numbering system. But just rearrange the parts so that they follow the ME-WE-GOD-YOU-WE paradigm. Now go back and add the ones you are missing.

Once you have done that, turn your paper over and see if you can think through your message one section at a time. I bet you can. People ask me all the time how I preach without looking at notes.

Now you know.

But don't tell anybody.

TAKEAWAY

- An outline built around your relationship with the audience, rather than the content, best matches the way they naturally process information.

- ME-WE-GOD-YOU-WE

- Begin writing these five words in the margin where they apply in your current way of outlining. Add the sections you are missing.

14

INTERNALIZE THE MESSAGE

What's your story?

Every communicator has notes. But there's no reason anybody has to know you have notes. Odds are, you want to become more conversational in your communication style. To do that, you can't be tied to your notes. The only people who converse with notes are people auditioning for a part in a play. But even the most amateur actors would never dream of walking out on stage with their script. Why? Because a good actor doesn't want to be caught acting. They want their audience to believe that they really are who they are pretending to be; that they really feel what they are pretending to feel; that the words they say come from their heart not a script. And we do, too!

There is a scene in *The Patriot* when Benjamin Martin, played by Mel Gibson, is saying goodbye to his five-year-old daughter, Susan, who hasn't spoken since her mom died. Throughout the movie, Martin has tried to cajole Susan into speaking. But to no avail.

Towards the end of the movie, Susan is standing next to her aunt Charlotte as Martin and his son Gabriel are preparing to ride off to do battle with the red coats. Just before mounting his horse Martin motions to Susan but she doesn't move. Then he kneels down and gently hugs her and says, "Just a little goodbye? One word? That's all I want to hear."

Susan remains silent, arms to her sides, unresponsive. Martin lets go and she just stares at him. But as Martin and Gabriel mount their horses and start to ride away, Susan, with tears streaming down her face, runs towards her father and cries out, "Papa! Papa, don't go, I'll say anything. Please, Papa, I'll say anything you want!"

Martin turns in his saddle and sees Susan running towards him. He yanks his horse around and begins galloping towards his little angel as she continues calling out. Grabbing her up into his arms, Martin holds her close as he fights back tears. "I'll talk to you," she cries, "I'll say anything you want, just tell me what you want me to say, I'll say anything, I promise, please, Papa just stay."

I saw The Patriot with a couple of friends that you may know, Reggie Joiner and Lanny Donoho. In the middle of that scene I glanced over at my buddies and they had tears running down their cheeks. Bunch of sissies. What's that about? It's a movie for heaven's sake. And it's Mel Gibson. And that's not even his actual daughter. They were crying as if they were witnessing a real miracle. And so did I. All six times I watched it. But how effective would that scene have been if little Susan kept glancing down at her notes as she read, "I'll talk to you. I'll say anything you want." Not very.

Now I realize acting and preaching are a bit different. But they are not as different as you might imagine. If you are on a stage with a microphone attached to you, you better be ready to perform. Like a good actor, you've got to be believable. After all, you actually believe! People are expecting you to engage them on multiple levels. And in light of what's at stake, you should be both engaging and convincing. If an actor is willing to memorize and internalize a script in order to convince you that he or she is someone other than who they really are, how motivated should we be to internalize our messages in order to convince our audience that we really are who we claim to be?

OWN IT

Before we stand (or in my case, sit) to deliver a message we must *own* it.

By *own* it I mean that you, the communicator, should be able to sit down at a table and communicate your message to an audience of two in a way that is both conversational and authentic. The message must in some way become a personal story you could tell as if drawing from personal experience. When you can "tell" your sermon rather than "preach" it, you are ready to communicate. But that won't happen until you have internalized it to the point where you could do a five-minute version from memory.

If that sounds unrealistic at this juncture it is probably because you are in the habit of squeezing too much information and too many verses and not enough life into your sermons. Information is difficult to memorize. Five passages from five different books of the Bible are hard to remember. Life on the other hand is neither difficult to memorize or hard to remember. By life I'm not talking just about personal illustrations, though I'm including those. I am talking about experiences that are common to people.

I find something very disingenuous about the speaker who says, "This is very, very important," and then reads something from his notes. Constantly referring to notes communicates, "I have not internalized this message. I want everybody else to internalize it, but I haven't." Consequently, I think every effective communicator must figure out how to internalize all of and memorize the majority of his or her message. No, not word-for-word, not a manuscript, not an outline, not verbatim. But somehow they need to be able to get up and deliver their message as a story.

Think about it, the only time anybody reads a story is when it isn't *their* story. You've never heard anybody who was nearly killed or seriously injured in a traffic accident pull out a manuscript and say, "Let me tell you what happened yesterday." You've never heard anybody open up a three-ring binder and say, "Let me tell you about my kids." Nobody recounts their son or daughter's championship soccer game with an outline in front of them. When people tell a personal story it's internalized. It flows like water from a stream. Sometimes it gushes like a river through a canyon. Either way, it comes from inside. The same should be true for those of us who claim to have the most important story in the world to tell. The story has changed us, and therefore the story has become part of our story. Somehow, it must be internalized. But that's not always easy. Especially when communicating is your weekly responsibility.

POINTLESS STORIES

Later in this chapter I'm going to give you several tips on how to use notes on the sly, but the two things that will help you most in this regard are things we have already talked about: One point messages and the ME-WE-GOD-YOU-WE approach to outlining. Creating one point messages makes internalizing a message much easier. Remembering one point is much easier than memorizing a bunch of points. Having one idea that everything else supports makes it easy to internalize a talk. When you have one strong point, the goal is to make your point, not cover everything in your notes. If you forget some supporting material but succeed in communicating your big idea, congratulations, you accomplished what you came to do. And let's face it, we are the only ones on the planet that know what we forgot to say. And if you are like most preachers, you probably have too much content to begin with. It is probably good that you left out some stuff. Besides, if you do multiple services, you will get another shot at it anyway.

THE BIG PIECES

When it comes to internalizing a message your outline is either your friend or your enemy; it either facilitates the internalization process or hampers it. One reason so many communicators don't think they can preach without notes is that their outline (or manuscript) overwhelms them. This is compounded by the fear of leaving something out or losing their place. But all of that can be resolved by adopting the approach to outlining we talked about in the previous chapter.

The secret is to reduce your entire message down to five or six pieces. Not points, pieces or sections or chunks of information. If you can remember the big pieces and the order in which they come, you are ready to go.

The big pieces serve as mental mile markers that allow you to keep moving and flag what's coming up next. When you run out of things to say about ME, you just move right on to WE. You may end up leaving some stuff out, but again, nobody will know but you. Remember, the goal is not to cover everything in your notes. It is to take your audience with you on a journey; to move them from mile marker to mile marker until you reach your destination.

When I'm coaching communicators, I'll often say, "What are the big pieces? Tell me the big pieces. Give me your introduction in one statement. What's next? What text are you using? Summarize the application. Give me your closing thought." When you can quickly review the five or six major pieces of the message in your head, chances are you are ready to communicate without being dependent on your notes.

The big pieces may vary in nature from message to message. You may want to organize the big pieces using the ME-WE-GOD-YOU-WE format. Or you may want to be more specific. Here are some examples:

Opening story—Question—Text—Application—Challenge

Opening question—Illustration—Text—Challenge—Application—Closing Story.

Introduction—Tension—Text—Visual—Application—Conclusion

Text—Question—Story—Text—Application

When preaching on the temptations of Christ, I opened the sermon by reading Matthew 4:1–2 where Matthew tells us that Jesus was led by the Holy Spirit into the wilderness to be tempted. How odd. I made a few comments on how strange that was, especially in light of the fact that Jesus specifically prayed, "lead us not into temptation." Then I talked about my struggle with temptation (ME) and how common it is for all of us (WE) then went back to the text to look at Jesus' response (God). I think it is great to begin with the text if there is something so odd or unbelievable that it immediately grabs people's attention. I do the same thing when I preach on the prodigal son. The opening statement in that trilogy of parables is that tax gatherers and sinners congregated to hear Him speak. How unusual. *People who were nothing like Jesus, liked Jesus.*

The point here is to identify the big pieces of your message and practice thinking through them. If you know the big pieces, the mile markers, you won't get lost. You will always know what's coming up next. When you run out of things to say about one, you just move on to the next one, knowing that you probably left something out. But again, you are the only one who knows.

TRICKS OF THE TRADE

As I mentioned earlier, there are ways to use notes without anyone knowing you are using notes. You don't need to memorize everything. With the ME-WE-GOD-YOU-WE approach, there are really only three big pieces you will need to commit to memory, and they are the easiest to remember anyway: ME, WE, and WE. These are the personal sections and these are probably the shortest sections. Best of all, these are the sections where if you accidentally leave something out it probably won't matter. But these are the sections I practice most. These are the sections I rehearse over and over in my head. After all, ME and WE is where we connect and engage the audience. WE is where we inspire them to do something with what they've heard. But between those two parts, there are plenty of opportunities to catch a stealth glimpse of our notes.

My guess is that you have already developed a system for writing comments and points into the margins of your Bible. And I imagine you have developed a skill for reading the text while glancing at what you have scribbled in the margins. A few years ago I abandoned the scribbling part and started cutting and pasting the text I am going to use out of a Bible program into a word processing document. That way I can actually print, rather than scribble, what I want to remember right into the text. Then I trim the pages so they fit into my Bible.

There are several advantages to this. To begin with, I am not limited to the space afforded me by my Bible margins. I can include more notes. That way I'm not bouncing back and forth from my Bible to my notes. It is seamless. Less distracting. And far easier for me.

At the end of my final text I print out a reminder of where I'm going from there. I may print a summary statement for the text I have read like we talked about in the last chapter. Or I may print something along the lines of, "There are three places where this applies." Or, "Here's what I think we should do with Jesus' words." Or if I'm moving from the text to a visual aid, I write "GO TO VISUAL."

The other advantage of printing the text is that on those rare occasions where I'm referencing more than one text, I don't have to find it in my Bible, it is already printed out. Then, when I'm finished I can file the printed text with my outline for future reference. I don't have to use the same Bible or rewrite all my notes in a different Bible if I want to repreach that message.

Another thing I do quite often is write out my main point on a three-by-five card and lay it beside my Bible. The reason I do is that my point is a statement I've spent some time crafting. I want to make sure I state it correctly. In the course of communicating a message it is not always easy for me to pull my statement from memory exactly as I have crafted it. Writing it out in big letters and setting it beside my Bible gives me a chance to glance down at it before I deliver it. Burying it in my notes or even in the text is too confusing. I like having it right there where I can't miss it.

There have been times when I realize I'm not going to get it right and I'll pick up the card and say something along the lines of, "This week while I was studying I wrote this statement." Then I'll read it. Having read it, I can usually repeat it a couple more times from memory. But I'm such a believer in the power of a well-crafted statement I would rather read it correctly than try to remember it and turn a clear point into a fuzzy one. I've learned that holding up a card and reading it has more impact than looking down at your notes and reading the same words. A single statement on a card communicates the importance of what you are reading. It is a visual way of underscoring the importance of what's being read.

But having said that, it is always best to have your main point committed to memory. As a general rule, don't use notes during those portions of a message that you want your audience to remember and internalize. This is why having your main idea committed to memory is so important. As we said earlier in this chapter, if you haven't internalized it, why should they? If you can't even remember the main thing, is it really that important?

My final memory aid comes to us from the wonderful world of technology. We have a video monitor on the front row facing the stage. Occasionally I will give the production team a short list of things to put on the monitor to jog my memory. Most of the time these are items that fall in the YOU section of the message. These are specific applications that I want to make sure I don't miss. It is much easier to glance down at a video monitor than it is to go scrambling back to my notes to find something. I have seen guys overuse this technology. They seemed as tied to their monitors as most communicators are to their notes. This electronic cheat sheet is no substitute for the hard work of memorization. But it sure makes life easier on those occasions when application #2 has slipped your mind. Sometimes I will ask our team to put my main idea on the monitor and just leave it up there during the entire message.

SAY IT OUT LOUD

I'm often asked if I practice my sermons. Yes and no. I never preach an entire message at home out loud. But there are portions I do rehearse out loud the night before. I always rehearse stories. By telling a story out loud I hear what is not clear and I bump into what is difficult to explain. At times I rehearse my stories at the dinner table and ask the fam for feedback.

The other portions I rehearse out loud are my introductions and conclusions. Our opening statements and closing statements are so important. If we don't engage our audience in the first few minutes, it is an uphill struggle from there. If we don't finish strong, an entire message may be forgotten before people get to their cars. Occasionally I will manuscript my introduction and conclusion. In my opinion, I think it is imperative that our opening and closing be committed to memory.

SATURDAY NIGHT

Here's how it works for me. I stay three weeks ahead in my preparation. On a given Thursday, when I head home from the office I will have the following three sermons completely finished. The advantage of staying ahead is, I'm ahead. If something interferes with my study time, no big deal, I'm still two weeks ahead. The other advantage is that it gives our production team plenty of time to create around the message.

The disadvantage of this approach is that when I pick up my outline on Saturday afternoon or evening I haven't looked at it in two or three weeks. So it looks like a lot of information to memorize and digest in a short amount of time.

I spend the first part of my Saturday study time simplifying. My goal on Saturday is to make it as memorable as possible. I'll look at a line or idea and think, *I'll never remember that*, and I cut it. When you are committed to internalizing the entire message you will be highly motivated to reduce it to the bare but essential minimum. And if you are only going to make *a* point, it is not hard to identify what to cut.

If something doesn't support, illustrate, or clarify the point, I cut it. I've been preaching long enough to get comfortable with the fact that I can fill up the time regardless of how much I cut. Most of the guys I coach pack their messages full of extra stuff in fear that they won't have enough to say. Then, invariably, they run out of time and are forced to rush their conclusion, which pretty much cancels out the impact of the entire sermon. Having too much to say has almost the same effect as saying nothing. Adding material in order to fill up time is a terrible approach. I understand the pressure. But think about it, do you have a tendency to go too short or too long? Besides, if you end early, nobody will complain. Field a few questions and then send everybody to lunch early. Bottom line, less is more.

A FINAL NOTE ON NOTES

I'm always amazed at how easy it is to retell the entire plot of a movie after having seen it once. And while I'm watching the movie I'm making no effort at all to remember anything. Stories are easy to remember and repeat. So are good sermons. Why? Because good sermons are like good movies or a good book. They engage you at the beginning by creating some kind of tension. They resolve that tension. There is a climax. And then there is a conclusion that ties up all the loose ends. Pretty simple. When you can reduce your message to a few big pieces it will read like a story. It will be memorable like a movie. People will wonder where the time went. But for that to happen you have to internalize it. It must become *your* story.

The other thing about a good movie is that the editor leaves a lot on the cutting room floor. At least that's what they did in the old days. That is, they take out a lot of good stuff so that the best stuff can shine. Not to mention, nobody wants to sit through a four-hour movie. To make our messages memorable for us and enjoyable for our audience we must discipline ourselves to do the same thing. It is better to be incomplete and engage your audience than to cover every little thing and be tied to your notes. If your audience isn't engaged, if they aren't tracking with you, does it really matter that you got everything in?

Memorize what must be memorized. Develop a method of referring to your notes that doesn't distract your audience from the message. Rethink the way you use the text. Look for opportunities to leave yourself reminders along the way. Internalize it.

TAKEAWAY

- Before you stand to deliver a message you must *own* it.

- Reduce your entire message down to five or six pieces. Not points, pieces or sections of information.

- If something doesn't support, illustrate, or clarify the point, cut it.

15

ENGAGE YOUR AUDIENCE

What's your plan to capture and keep their attention?

If communication can be compared to taking people on a journey, then it is imperative that we actually *take them with us*. If you have ever sat through a presentation of any kind and counted ceiling tiles or played mental games or worked on your to do list it is probably because the presenter had broken a fundamental rule of communication. They drove off and left you standing at the station. They failed to engage you and keep you engaged.

Not too long ago I was visiting a church with some friends. As I sat there trying to pay attention, I noticed that I was not alone in my struggle. There were probably three or four hundred people in the auditorium. It was evident that the pastor had gone to great lengths to prepare his message. But it was equally evident that the majority of the audience was not engaged. In spite of what seemed obvious to me, he went right on, presenting his material. In fact, he seemed to be so engrossed in his presentation that I'm not sure it really mattered to him that the majority of his audience had checked out. Not only did he leave the station without anybody on board, he didn't seem to notice or care.

When the service concluded we went to lunch. There were about twelve of us. After lunch we hung out until late in the afternoon. Not once did anybody mention the sermon. It was as if it never happened. Now, I'm sure nobody noticed this but me. But it bothered me so much that I still think about it. This pastor spent hours preparing a sermon, presented it, and it made such little impact that a group of Christians walked out and never made a single comment about what they just experienced. Granted, I didn't bring it up either. Primarily because I couldn't think of anything good to say. How tragic. But how common.

So how do we make sure our audience is with us? How do we engage an audience and keep them engaged throughout our presentation? Before we dive into some specifics, I want to review a basic principle. A principle that every world-class ad agency and film-maker has embraced but one that doesn't always sit well in the religious community. Here it is: *Presentation trumps information when it comes to engaging the audience.* Another way to state the same principle is: *Attention and retention is determined by presentation, not information.* Presentation matters. A lot.

P/I

How you say what you say is as important as *what* you say. Presentation determines your audience's attention span. There's a lot of talk these days about people's attention span. The theory is that it is getting shorter and shorter because of technology and options. But I don't buy it. *Lord of the Rings* was how long? Not only did my kids and I sit through each of those flicks twice at the theater, we bought 'em all and watched again at home. They ended the same way every time but we watched again anyway. *King Kong* lasted all day. My thirteen-year old and I saw that twice. Every kid I know can sit in front of an Xbox or PS2 (soon to be 3) for hours without being distracted. Most adults can lose themselves in a good book. The point is, when we are engaged, time flies. When we are not engaged time stands still. The issue is not the *span* of people's attention. The issue is our ability to capture and hold people's attention.

Somewhere we bought into the notion that good content was all that is required to engage an audience. That is rarely the case. I say *rarely* because there are occasions in which information alone can capture and keep people's attention. These rare occasions actually underscore the point of this chapter. And we will get to that in a page or two. But in most cases, presentation is what captures and keeps people's attention.

Think about your favorite restaurant for a moment. My guess is that they serve beef, chicken, and fish. So does mine! That's amazing. We are thinking about the same restaurant!

The thing that makes your favorite restaurant your favorite is not the animals they serve or the plants they suggest you eat with the animals they serve. What makes it your favorite is the way they prepare and present those animals and plants. Their presentation and preparation is what keeps you coming back for more. The same can be said for communication. It's our preparation and presentation that will keep people engaged.

I saw a great illustration of this when one of our staff presented a familiar Old Testament Bible story three times in a row to the same group of kids within a fifteen minute time frame. She had everything working against her. To begin with, the audience was a mix of first through fifth graders. Most of the kids already knew the story. And these kids had just come from their small groups where they had been in a learning environment for over an hour. At the end of her third time through the story the kids gave her a standing ovation. They were engaged from start to finish. How did she do it?

First she had a group of actors act out the story. Then she had the same actors present it again as a silent film. Then she asked them to do the story as if it were an opera. It was amazing. My eleven-year old said it was the funniest thing he had ever seen. When I asked him to tell me the point of the story he shot back, "It was about resourcefulness. Resourcefulness is using what you have to get a job done."

Often we think we need *new* content to keep people engaged. Not true. We need fresh presentations. Let's face it, it's always Moses who comes down from the mountain with the Ten Commandments. David kills Goliath every time. Daniel never gets eaten by the lions. John the Baptist never escapes from Herod's dungeon. Jesus is born in a stable. The stories don't change. The variable is our presentation. Two communicators can tell the same story with two completely different results. It is all in the presentation.

PUSH BACK

"But wait," you say, "doesn't God's Word stand on its own? Does presentation really matter when it comes to the Scriptures? I would answer no to the first question and yes to the second. And here's why. Drive over to your local Korean church and ask them for a copy of the Bible in Korean. Spend an hour or so reading through and meditating on the Korean Scriptures. Now, if you can read Korean, that might be a very profitable exercise. If you can't, it won't. Why? Because a Korean presentation of God's Word to a person who can't read Korean is neither engaging nor helpful. Presentation matters.

Not convinced? Think about it this way.

The apostle John writes, "In the beginning was the Word, and the Word was with God..."[9]

As long as the Word was *with* God it didn't really do us much good did it? We know that to be the case because of what follows.

"The Word became flesh and made his dwelling among us."[10]

Why? Wasn't it enough that there was a Word? Did it (or He) really need to show up among us? Absolutely. When the Word became flesh and dwelt among us, that's when the impact was felt.

He continues.

"We have seen his glory, the glory of the One and Only, who came from the Father, full of grace and truth."[11]

The world was *presented* when Jesus, the Word, showed up clothed in humanity.

"No one has ever seen God, but God the One and Only, who is at the Father's side, has made him known."[12]

Jesus *presented* the Father to the world. Creation presented the glory of God. Jesus presented a side of God that nobody had seen until the Son made it known. This became most evident in a conversation between Jesus and Phillip. Phillip, in what was probably a moment of frustration, asked Jesus to show him the Father. Like many of us, he wanted to see, or at least catch a glimpse of God. Remember Jesus' answer?

"Don't you know me, Philip, even after I have been among you such a long time? Anyone who has seen me has seen the Father. How can you say, 'Show us the Father'?"[13] His point? Phillip, seeing Me is as close as you will ever get in this lifetime to seeing the Father.

My point? Jesus was a necessary expression and presentation of the Father. God wasn't satisfied with the fact of His existence. He wanted to be presented in a way that allowed His prize creation to understand and embrace Him. Some did. Some did not. But the presentation was there for all to see. God went to great lengths to make Himself known to this world. Seems to me we should be willing to do the same thing. Jesus was the living Word. Shouldn't we do all we can to make the written Word come alive for our audience? I think so.

I'm sure grateful for men and women who brought it to life for me when I was a disinterested teenager. I owned a Bible. But it didn't own me. God's Word was living. But for all practical purposes, it wasn't living in me. Then one summer a guy named Dan Dehaan showed up at camp and captured my attention through his *presentation* of the Scriptures. I was so impacted that I began reading the Bible on my own for the first time. I've been reading it ever since. Dan is one of the reasons I'm in ministry. I spent fifteen years teaching the Bible to teenagers. Thanks to Dan, I never once assumed that it was enough to just *preach* the Word. My responsibility was to *present* the word in a way that engaged my audience.

In the first century people loved or hated Jesus. But nobody fell asleep. He was engaging and enraging. He pulled out all the stops when it came to communicating the truth and nature of the Father. He didn't simply speak. He spoke with authority. There was a marked difference between Him and the other teachers of His day. He was creative, direct, compassionate, and offensive. He was the master communicator. People who were nothing like Him, liked Him. Sinners and tax gatherers flocked to hear Him. On several occasions, thousands gathered to listen. He had a limited amount of time to communicate *the* most important message that would ever be delivered to this world. And He communicated it in such a fashion that His word pictures and parables have laced the literature of every generation since. Read the gospels. Jesus wasn't content with being right. He was committed to being heard. So how can those of us who feel called to leverage His words to impact our generation be content with anything less?

In this next section I am going to address a facet of communication that may appear to be in conflict with what I have said thus far in this chapter. But these two ideas actually work together as we will discover a little later.

WHEN INFORMATION *IS* ENOUGH

I mentioned earlier that there are some rare occasions when presentation is not important because the information itself is so engaging. I'll give you an example. A couple of years ago I had an MRI. A closed MRI. Those are a lot of fun. On the way home I called Sandra and told her I definitely wanted to be cremated.

Actually, I called my doctor to see when I could come and let him tell me what he ascertained from my pictures. His assistant informed me that he didn't have any openings for a week! That seemed like an eternity. Why? Because I believed he had some information that was vital for me. When my appointment date finally rolled around I got there early. And when he walked through the door he had my undivided attention. In that environment, presentation was irrelevant. I was there for the information. I'm sure you've had similar experiences.

This brings us to a very important communication principle. The more interested we are in a topic, the easier it is to engage us with the information. I showed up at the doctor's office with a high level of interest. He didn't have to do anything to create interest in me. But why? Why was I so interested in his information?

I was interested because I was convinced my doctor had the answer to a question I was dying to have answered. I was interested because there was a tension I believed he could resolve for me. I was interested because I had a problem I was hoping he would be able to solve. Tension creates a hunger for information.

Now, imagine this. What if after finishing with me he had said, "Hey Andy, would you be *interested* in hanging out in the office with me while I go over MRIs with my other patients? The answer would have been, No, I'm not really *interested.* Like a lot of churchgoers I might have stuck around to be polite. But would I be *interested?* Not really. After all, what does someone else's MRI have to do with ME?

Presentation takes a backseat to information when an audience is absolutely convinced that you are about to answer a question they've been asking, solve a mystery they have been unable to solve, or resolve a tension they have been unable to resolve.

When Atlanta hosted its first Gay Rights parade back in the 80's I was working for my dad in mid-town Atlanta. As it turned out, we were on the parade route. Not only that, the parade was scheduled for Sunday morning. As you can imagine, it was a big deal. A really big deal. A couple of weeks before the big day, I suggested to my dad that he ought to preach on what the Bible has to say about homosexuality. As it turned out, he was finishing a series the Sunday morning of the parade and then leaving town that afternoon. He suggested I do it. Being twenty-seven and not knowing any better, I agreed. On the Sunday morning of the parade he announced to the congregation that I was going to speak that night on the subject of what the Bible has to say about homosexuality.

Needless to say, I didn't have to work very hard at being engaging. Everybody was engaged. Especially those from the gay community who decided to join us for the evening. Why? Because everybody assumed I was going to answer a question they had, resolve a tension they carried, or perhaps make a total fool of myself. Any of those three was worth a trip to church. I've long since taken that tape out of circulation. Tape? You remember those, don't you?

My point is, there are topics so controversial, unusual, or emotional that the information alone will engage an audience. When I announce that I'm going to talk about sex, we have high attendance Sunday. We did a weekend on the subject of pornography. It was standing room only. When everybody knew I was going to preach on divorce, the place was packed.

But let's face it, there's just a handful of subjects where the information is so engaging that the presentation is secondary. And even with those topics, presentation still matters. It just doesn't matter as much.

RAISING THE NEED

I have two reasons for spending so much time on this. First, it's true. Second, these rare occasions illustrate an important principle. People engage easily when they are convinced that you are about to answer a question they've been asking, solve a mystery they have been unable to solve, or resolve a tension they have been unable to resolve. When an audience knows ahead of time that you are going to do one of those three things they show up interested. They might even show up early. They are emotionally engaged as soon as you walk up on the stage. But what if the topic is not emotionally charged? What if no one even knows what you are going to talk about? What if your audience shows up with no sense of anticipation?

Simply put, you have to manufacture interest. On the average Sunday morning, or whenever you communicate, your first responsibility is to pose a question your audience wants answered, create a tension they need resolved, or point to a mystery they have been unable to solve. And if you launch into your message before you do one of those three things, chances are, you will leave them standing at the station.

If we give answers to questions no one is asking or attempt to resolve a tension that no one is feeling, then our information is likely to fall on deaf ears. Information that does not address a felt need is perceived as irrelevant. It may actually be incredibly relevant, but if our audience doesn't see or feel the need for it, it is perceived as irrelevant. No one is engaged. They may sit quietly until we are finished talking. But they will not be engaged.

Implication?

Your introduction may be the most important part of your message. It is the equivalent to a railroad conductor yelling, "All aboard!" Or in my case, it is the equivalent of standing beside our SUV, yelling,

"Load up, we are leaving." The introduction should provide listeners with a reason to listen. Your introduction should raise the question you are going to answer, create the tension you are going to resolve, or point to the mystery you are going to solve. My impression is that many communicators, especially preachers, are so anxious to get into the body of their message they spend little time preparing their introductions. They leave the station alone.

INTRODUCTIONS

I usually write my introduction last. Often, I rewrite my introduction on Saturday night. It is not unusual for my introduction to take up three-quarters of a page in my typical three-page outline. It is the one section of my messages I always practice out loud. My assumption is, if I don't capture the audience's attention in the first five minutes, all is lost. My hours of preparation are for naught. My life-changing insights won't change anybody.

Here are three pairs of questions I recommend you refer to as you develop your introductions:

- What is the question I am answering? What can I do to get my audience to want to know the answer to that question?
- What is the tension this message will resolve? What can I do to make my audience feel that tension?
- What mystery does this message solve? What can I do to make my audience want a solution?

I believe every message can be organized around one of these three dynamics. Recognizing the one that best fits your message will give you insight into how to approach your introduction. When you have succeeded in narrowing the focus of your message to one central idea, it makes choosing an approach to your introduction much easier.

Jesus did this all the time. "Who do men say that I am?" That certainly surfaced some tension. He was constantly throwing out statements that were so contrary to the assumptions of the day that He immediately had everybody's attention. "Blessed are the poor in spirit." That's not right. The goal is to be rich in spirit, isn't it? His parables highlighted the tension between the kingdom of heaven and the kingdom of man. How about this as an introduction: "You have heard it said...but I say..."?

Jesus launched a discussion one day with this statement "I tell you the truth, it is hard for a rich man to enter the kingdom of heaven. Again I tell you, it is easier for a camel to go through the eye of a needle than for a rich man to enter the kingdom of God."[14] Remember the response? "When the disciples heard this, they were greatly astonished and asked, "Who then can be saved?"[15] He led them to ask the question He wanted to answer.

If you are successful in creating tension through your introduction you will also have been successful in surfacing some emotion. Emotionally charged environments are engaging. You pay attention when there is tension. Have you ever been scuba diving or parachuting? If so, I bet you were very much engaged in the instructor's instructions. That same dynamic holds true whenever we stand up to speak. Tension gains attention. If we fail to create tension we are wrong to assume that we will capture and keep anyone's attention.

This is why in chapter 13 I warned you not to transition from WE to the next section until you feel like you have created a tension that your audience is dying for you to resolve. In other words, assume no interest. Focus on the question you are intending to answer until you are confident your audience wants it answered. Otherwise you are about to spend twenty or thirty minutes of your life answering a question nobody is asking.

But as you know, grabbing your audience's attention with a carefully crafted introduction is just the beginning. You need to keep them engaged the whole way through. So here are five suggestions to help you keep your audience engaged past the introduction.

RULES OF ENGAGEMENT

1. Check your speed.

The human brain can process words much faster than the mouth can produce them. This one insight has huge implications for communicators. Jeff Miller, in a piece he wrote for *Leadership* magazine, talks about a communicator's WPMs—Words Per Minute. According to Jeff, the average rate of speech for English-speaking Westerners is 150 per minute. "Studies have shown," Miller says, "that speaking slightly above 150 words per minute adds an element of dignity to one's message. Faster speakers—up to 190 words per minute—were rated as more objective, knowledgeable, and persuasive than slower speakers."

Bottom line, if you talk too slow, you will be perceived as boring, regardless of how important your content is. Jeff goes on to point out that public speakers need to increase their speed to a number that exceeds normal conversation. Otherwise, people's brains will get so far ahead of what we're saying that the lag time will drive them crazy. They will disengage. Chances are, you have been forced to sit and listen to someone who spoke so slowly that you felt like the life was just being drained out of you. Again, it probably wasn't the significance of what he or she was saying, it was their pace.

Your WPMs communicate your interest in and passion for your topic. When one of my kids comes running down the hall talking a mile a minute, I'm engaged before I even know what they are talking about. Their pace is fast enough to make me believe that they have something important to say. The pace of our words communicates the importance of our words.

If you listen to your own tapes or CDs and find yourself wanting to press fast forward, you may have a WPM issue. If you aren't in the habit of listening to your own messages, you have another issue. More on that later.

I have a WPM issue to contend with. But it is not a problem with talking too slow. I have a tendency to talk way too fast. After my first seminary classroom sermon my professor blurted out, "Andy, if you don't slow down you will be completely ineffective as a communicator." I've never forgotten that. Actually, it is one of the few things I still remember about seminary. But he was right. One of the main reasons I listen to my own sermons is to monitor my speed. Talking too fast can wear people out just like talking too slow. Not to mention the fact that it wreaks havoc with my diction. If people have to think too hard to follow us, eventually they will quit following. It's exhausting. And talk about exhausting, imagine what it does to the poor folks who sign for our deaf congregation. I'm surprised their hands don't catch on fire. On more than one occasion I've put a three-by-five card in my Bible that reads, *slow down!*

2. Slow down in the curves.

It is easy to lose people in the curves. As you transition from introduction to the text to your point to your application, give people some sort of indication that you are making a transition. Let your audience know you are making a transition. Let everybody know you are making a transition. Yes, I just repeated myself twice. That's one way of letting people know you are moving to a different section of your message. Saying something one time doesn't highlight it. Saying the same thing a couple of different ways, does. Here's a typical transition I use when moving from WE to GOD.

Fortunately for us, we are not the first group to wonder about this. Men and women in the first century shared our concern. So much so that one day a group came to Jesus and actually asked Him about it. So for the next few minutes we have the opportunity of listening to Jesus address this very issue. And once again, we are reminded of how relevant the Bible is to the issues we struggle with today.

Here's a transition statement I used when moving from the text to the application section of a message.

Now, in light of all that, what should we do? How does this principle intersect with our lives? What do you do with this tomorrow morning when you show up at the office or school? What does this look like around the dinner table? Here are a few suggestions.

Notice in this second paragraph I have not suggested any specific applications. I just let everybody know what's coming next. When preparing an outline I always write out my transitions as I have here. These transition paragraphs in my outline serve as a visual reminder to me of my need to slow down in the curves.

Transitions give people a chance to catch back up with you. They provide the audience with an opportunity to rejoin the discussion. They may have lost track of where you are for a variety of reasons, many of which you may have no control over. But by slowing down in the curves; by creating a break in the action, they are able to reengage.

3. Navigate through the text.

In chapter 13 I made the observation that it is the textual part of most messages where things tend to bog down. My feeling is, the text should be the *most* engaging part of the message. But that requires some work on our part. Here are my rules of the road when it comes to engaging people with the text.

- Have the audience turn to one passage and one passage only. You may throw a couple of others up on the screen, but don't expect your audience to be able to follow you as you gallop through the Bible. Pick a central text and teach it. It is better for people to understand one verse than to have turned to four verses.
- Don't read long sections without comment. Comment along the way. Even in narratives, don't read the entire story and then begin your sermon. Lead people through the text.
- Highlight and explain odd words or phrases. Think of yourself as a navigator or tour guide. Point things out as you go...but keep moving.
- Voice your frustration or skepticism about the text. If it frustrates you, it is frustrating someone in your audience. If it sounds unreasonable or impractical to you, you are not alone. Whenever you can say what your audience is thinking, your audience will consider you believable and approachable.

"That's just hard to believe, isn't it?"

"If God would allow me to erase a verse, this might be it."

"Obviously Jesus has never met your boss."

"If I was one of the disciples I might have walked at that point."

"This is where we want to raise our hand and tell our sad story. After all, if God knew what you had been through, you would get a pass."

- Help the audience anticipate the main point of the text.

"Okay, get ready, here it is…"

"Then He drops the bomb."

"At this point Jesus' audience is wondering, 'What the heck is He talking about.' Then He tells 'em…"

- Deliberately read the text wrong, inserting a word that means the opposite and then pause to let it sink in.

"As it is written, it is more blessed to receive than to give."

"Husbands, love your wives in the same manner that they love you."

"For by *consistency* you are saved."

- Have the audience read certain words out loud for emphasis.

"And the truth shall make you…what? What's the word? Say it with me."'

"If we confess our sins, He is faithful and just and will… What's the word? Forgive. He will forgive us our sins and purify us from all unrighteousness."

"You have heard that it was said, Love your neighbor and hate your enemy. But I tell you... What's the next word? Love. Can you believe it? Love your enemies and pray for those who persecute you?"

- Summarize the text with a well-crafted statement. Remember, you have promised to address the tension, felt need, question, issue, whatever it is you established up front. Make sure your time in the text actually does that. A pre-prepared and memorized summary statement will insure that you don't accidentally leave the text without making it clear why you were in the text to begin with. That happens frequently in sermons. We think we've made it clear because we've been discussing the text for ten minutes. But covering the text is no guarantee that we've clearly communicated the point of the text.

"Paul's point is that since Christ forgave us, we are to forgive one another."

"Joseph simply did what anyone in His circumstances would do who was confident that God was with him."

"When Peter acted on his faith, he recognized who Christ was."

- Use visuals every chance you get. Visuals are engaging. Even bad ones. If you are preaching on the great commission, get a map. If you are preaching on David and Goliath, get a slingshot. If you are explaining Jesus' insights on the relationship between our hearts and our money, bring some cash. Make a big heart.

One time I was teaching through the verses pertaining to our individual roles in the body of Christ. I got several big glass containers, filled them with yellow water and put one rubber body part in each. Then I covered each one with a cloth. (By the way, when you have stuff on stage covered with a sheet, you are already ahead of the guy down the street before you even start preaching.)

Anyway, it looked like something out of a horror movie. When I pulled the covers off people thought they were real. I explained that that's how God viewed Christians who refused to act as part of the body. Detached body parts are gross.

Everybody was engaged. Nauseated, but engaged.

- Resist the urge to share everything you have learned in your research. I always have a half page or more of interesting stuff that I love too much to trash but know better than to try and cram into the sermon. If it doesn't facilitate the journey, cut it. If it doesn't help your audience resolve the tension, save it. After all, you've still got YOU and WE to cover. And the last thing you want to do is rush through your conclusion. A hard landing leaves the passengers feeling a bit uneasy. The same is true of a rushed conclusion to a message.

Bottom line: *Engage the audience with the text.* Don't just read it and move on. Don't get lost in the minutia. We want people to love God's Word. Engage them with it.

4. Add something unexpected to the trip.

The unexpected is always engaging. Always. If you have ever had someone pass out during a service or had a bird fly into your meeting room you know what I'm talking about. When something unusual happens, everybody is interested. So why not leverage this maxim to your advantage? Plan something unusual.

Not too long ago, Jeff Henderson, the campus pastor at our Buckhead Campus leveraged this principle in a remarkably creative way. Buckhead Church is our video campus. Ordinarily, there is no live speaker, the audience watches a video. There are occasions when we need to have a live communicator. The first Sunday of the year is one of those occasions.

Jeff volunteered to kick the year off with a message entitled, "Life Interrupted." Since interruption was the theme, he decided to stage one. The service started as it usually does. After the offering, the screen dropped and I appeared and began preaching. About five minutes into the service, Jeff and his crew faked a power outage. Everything went dark, including the screens. At that point, Jeff walked up and delivered an amazing message on what to do when life is interrupted. Everybody was engaged. It was incredible. In fact, it was so well done, about half the audience really believed the power went out and Jeff just happened to have a message prepared.

Granted, that was pretty extreme. But there are plenty of things you can do short of a power outage to challenge the predictability of your speaking environment. Visuals accomplish the same thing. So do interviews, banter with an audience member, bringing people up on the stage, letting someone draw or paint while you speak. One morning I sat down at the piano and played a short song I wrote that emphasized the point of the message. It was terrible. But everybody was engaged.

I would imagine that you have missed dozens of opportunities to apply this principle simply because you didn't think about it. You were happy to have an outline. Whose got energy left to plan something unexpected? Here's a suggestion. Get somebody else to think about it. Pull a team together at the beginning of your next series, give 'em your big idea and then assign them the task of helping you spice things up.

My prediction is that they will come up with a bunch of really bad ideas, one of which can be tweaked into a good one. Over time they will gain a sense of what you are comfortable with, and what just won't work for you. Bottom line, look for opportunities to introduce the unexpected. No one will be expecting it.

5. Take the most direct route.

In short, *be direct.* Your audience needs to know where you are going early in the journey. No doubt you have experienced the frustration of being ten or twelve minutes into a presentation and thinking to yourself, "Where is this going?" Now stop and think about that for a moment.

If you were to have the audacity to actually stand up and shout out to the communicator, "Hey buddy, where are you going with all of this?" Two things would take place. Well, maybe three, if you include being thrown out. The first thing that would happen is the communicator would be surprised that you don't know. Because in his or her mind it is perfectly clear where the message is heading. The second thing that would happen is that the speaker would probably tell you precisely where it was heading, to which you may respond, "Well then why didn't you just tell us that to begin with?"

So where am *I* going with this? Err on the side of being too direct when it comes to orienting your audience to the question you are going to answer, the tension you want to resolve, or the mystery you want to help them solve. Get there quicker than you think you need to. And be more specific than you think you need to. And repeat it more times than you think you need to. They want to know what you are going to talk about. They want to know where you are going as soon as you begin talking. The longer you hold them off, the greater risk you run of having them disengage.

I was a journalism major in college. That may come as a shock. I hope not. I had a professor named Dr. Davis. He was great. One of his favorite things to do was call students to the front, read the opening paragraph of their story, and ask, "What are you trying to say here?" On most occasions, the student under fire would rattle off a very cohesive and direct summary of the opening paragraph. Then Dr. Davis would hand the paper back and say, "Then say it."

Like you, I've sat through too many messages where I wanted to stand up and say, "What are you trying to say?" I'm sure they knew. But I didn't know. And they weren't helping me. They were dancing all around their idea but wouldn't just come out and state it. Very frustrating. Worse than that, they had no clue as to the frustration they were creating in their audience. As a general rule, it is better to tell your audience what you are going to talk about before you begin talking about it. Otherwise, they have no context, no frame of reference, for the information you are giving them.

If you run across a topic or narrative that merits a more indirect approach, then do your audience a favor and let them know that you know that the message doesn't appear to be going anywhere. A simple, "Hang with me, this is going somewhere" will allow all the super linear people to relax. Sneaking up on a topic through the back door is a wonderful communication technique. But there is an art to keeping an audience engaged while you lead them through the dark. If you have credibility with an audience they will trust that your seemingly random information is all going to come together in the end. But for the average communicator, direct is better.

LISTEN AND LEARN

Some communicators are more naturally engaging than others. But we can all improve. You can become more engaging. Next time you hear someone who you just can't get enough of, ask yourself why. Why are they so easy to listen to? What are they doing or not doing that makes the time fly and the information so accessible? And next time you find yourself counting ceiling tiles and flipping through your Bible waiting for the speaker to stop speaking, ask yourself the same question. Make a list of everything they are doing wrong. Ask yourself what they could have done to make their message work. Rewrite their talk the way you would have delivered it. Then go up afterwards and hand it to them. They will appreciate it. Probably take you to dinner.

Remember, listening is not like reading. If you are reading and lose your place or lose track of the story line, you can back up and read it again. But if you get lost in a verbal presentation, chances are you are lost till the end. So do what it takes to keep your audience with you. Your message is important. Besides, you spent hours putting it together. Don't leave people standing at the station, load 'em up before you leave. And don't lose 'em in your transitions, slow down. And please don't let 'em bail out in the middle of the text. Navigate them through the Scriptures. Take a few risks. Try some new things. Engage your audience.

TAKEAWAY

- Engage your audience.

- Engage your audience.

- Engage your audience.

16

FIND YOUR VOICE

What works for you?

I mentioned up front that you might find yourself wondering, *Isn't this just one way of communicating? Isn't Andy just writing about his style of communication? Don't we need to develop our own style and approach?* I get questions like these every time I talk about communication. So let's talk about style.

Much has been written on the importance of *being yourself* as a communicator. And I would agree. Authenticity communicates volumes. Authenticity covers a multitude of communication sins. If a communicator is believable and sincere, I can put up with a lot of things. But if I get the feeling that I'm listening to their stage personality, big turnoff. I imagine you are the same way. I want to hear *you*, not your best rendition of your favorite communicator.

I love what Chuck Swindoll says about this:

Know who you are.

Accept who you are.

Be who you are.[16]

I think that is great advice for the man who thinks he needs to mimic Rick Warren or the woman who accessorizes herself in an attempt to be the next Beth Moore. But "be who you are" can become an excuse. My *style* can become a smoke screen for any number of bad communication habits. Through the years I've heard too many preachers and teachers play the style card to keep from having to change and improve. Boring is not a style. Boring is boring. Confusing may be a style. But it is still confusing. Each of our communication habits, both good and bad, are part of our style. But bad habits need to be eliminated from our style, not defended as part of it. "Being who you are," to borrow from Chuck's quote, is not an excuse for poor communication skills. It is an exhortation to be who God made you rather than trying to be who God made somebody else. It is not the same as saying:

Know that your messages are too complicated.

Accept that they are too complicated.

Be complicated!

Or,

Know that you aren't engaging.

Accept that you aren't engaging.

Be unengaging!

Be who you are. But be the very best communicator *you* can possibly be. To do that you must be willing to sacrifice what's comfortable—what has become part of your style—for the sake of what is effective. And over time the changes you make will become part of your style. Perhaps a few illustrations will help.

PRINCIPLE AND STYLE

Years ago a very well-known communicator was passing through town so I invited him to stay with us. This is a guy who travels and speaks for a living. He's booked solid eighteen to twenty months out. He told me one year he spoke over four hundred times. He does everything from student camps to Bible conferences to revivals. He sells lots of product. He's creative, funny, and naturally engaging.

As we were sitting in my kitchen talking, the subject of communication came up. He started asking me questions about how and when I prepared. How far out I planned. Typical preacher questions. I felt like he might be open to some new ideas so I took a chance. "I think I can help you with something," I said.

He smiled, "Really? What's that?"

I continued, "I've noticed a pattern in your communication that you may not be aware of. When you get to the Bible part of your messages, I always sense a decline in the momentum. It is like you are two different communicators. On the front and back end you are funny, relevant, and engaging. Once you dive into the text you get a bit preachy. And honestly, I don't think you connect your topic to the text very well."

Once again he smiled. "I've noticed the same thing," he said. I asked him to pull out a message I had recently heard him give. He had it with him. In fact, he was planning to give it again the following night in a different city. Like most preachers, when he got to the text he felt the need to cover three or four points. In this case he had four. So I suggested he reduce it to one. He looked at me like most guys do at this point. His eyes said it all. *How am I going to fill the time?* I assured him that would not be a problem.

He laughed. "You're right. That's never the problem." We spent about thirty minutes reorganizing his message around *a* point instead of four. By the time we were finished his nervousness had changed to excitement. "I wish somebody had told me about this a long time ago."

Two days later he called me. "It went great," he said. "I felt like my momentum actually picked up when I got to the text. It was so much easier this way. I don't think I even used my notes."

Here's my point. He did not alter his style. He simply incorporated a principle; one idea is better than four. He didn't quit being himself, he just adjusted his approach. And by his own admission it needed to be adjusted. He would agree that the way he handled the text actually worked against his style. But his adjustment wasn't an attempt to copy or emulate anybody else. In fact, he is a communicator many communicators try to emulate. Like most of us, he inherited a style of communication that he is committed to breaking away from. The last vestige was the four-point outline where every point received equal treatment.

I have another friend, not as well known, who because of a particular area of expertise is in great demand in the arena of church leadership. I think I've heard every talk he's given on this particular topic. But I noticed two bad habits. He rarely made transition statements. Consequently, it is just about impossible to know when he has changed subjects or moved on to the next part of his talk. Suddenly, you realize, "Oh, he's talking about something different." He would leave it to the audience to connect the dots. Like most bad communication habits, he was totally unaware of what he was doing. That is, until he asked me for a critique. I have so much respect for this gentleman that I felt funny critiquing him about anything. But I got over it.

We went through one of his outlines, and I drew lines between the different sections and said, "You are going around these curves way too fast. You've got to slow down and tell us that you are moving on to the next section. Otherwise, you lose your audience in the transitions." Again, this had nothing to do with style. I was simply pointing out a principle of communication. Namely, slow down in the curves. When you transition between parts of a talk, throw in a few lines of transition so people can follow.

His other bad habit was that he would ends his talks too abruptly. The way I described it to him was that when he brought the car to a stop I felt like he was throwing me into the windshield. Without any verbal or nonverbal warning he would say, "Let's pray." That's when you realized he was through. But there was no lead in. No signals that he was bringing his talk to a close.

"Come to a stop slowly," I said. "Manuscript your closing thoughts so that you don't have to think so much about *what* you are saying. That way you can concentrate on your pace and the emotion of the moment." The other thing I suggested was that he pause after his closing statement before he launched into a closing prayer.

He was so grateful. After going back and listening to a couple of his talks he called me and said, "I see what you mean. I think I have become so familiar with my material that I don't really think about transitions. And you are definitely right about the way I close. It is way too abrupt." These were minor adjustments that in no way affected his *style* of communication. He didn't need to change his style. He just needed to tweak a couple of things.

One of the most difficult conversations I've ever had was with a preacher who would never stay within the time he was allotted. I was working for my dad when this occurred. The last time this fellow preached for us we were very clear about the time constraints and how there was no room for error because of our parking situation. He said he understood and then went twenty minutes over in both services.

The temptation, of course, was just not to invite him back and let that be the end of it. But I felt like he should know why we never invited him again. So I took him to lunch. I was thirty-five and he was closing in on fifty. I was a student pastor. He traveled and spoke internationally. He was big-time. I was still taking kids to Six Flags on the weekends. Halfway through lunch I told him we weren't going to have him back and why. He was shocked. I asked him if anyone had ever told him that he had a reputation for ignoring his time constraints and wreaking havoc with schedules. No one had ever told him. His defense was, "When I'm speaking I believe I'm being led by the Holy Spirit. I just go with my leading."

I humbly shared with him that I didn't buy it. I went on to explain that I believed the Holy Spirit was at work in every facet of what happened on Sunday morning; preschool, middle school, parking lot, etc. Furthermore, I believed the Holy Spirit was active in our planning for what happened during our weekend services and that He was actually working against the Holy Spirit.

At that point he became a bit defensive. I would have, too.

While we were on the subject, I went on to share with him that I thought his messages would be far more effective if he shortened them. By the time he arrived at his conclusion everybody was thinking about the time, their kids, or lunch. He consistently missed the optimal window for making his point. On two occasions we had to cancel the closing song because he went so long. I told him about that and asked him how he thought that made the musicians feel who had spent hours preparing.

By the time I finished he was ready to write apology notes. I told him that wouldn't be necessary. What I didn't tell him was that everybody was so frustrated with him I'm not sure they would have been received all that well. Last I heard, he was still ignoring the clock. It's part of his style. And it's rude.

Don't dismiss principles of communication in defense of style. If you want to be an effective communicator, you must allow communication principles to *shape* your style. At the end of the day, principles win out over style. For example, in 1984, while in seminary, my Hebrew professor was asked to speak in chapel. He was new to the school. He was young, cocky, aloof, and as you might imagine, he was not particularly liked. He was only there a couple of years before being asked to move on. When I heard he was doing chapel I almost didn't go.

In four years of seminary his message is the only one I can remember. But it had nothing to do with his style or his presentation. Both were lacking. He was dry, he read his sermon, he made little to no eye contact. He stood behind the lectern during the entire message. And to cap it all off, he was teaching out of the Old Testament and read from his Hebrew text, which we all interpreted as showing off. But in spite of everything he had working against him, I remember his message to this day. Why? Because he made one and only one point. And he made it unmistakably clear. He didn't illustrate it. He didn't have any visuals. Nobody came out after him and punctuated his point with a song. He told us up front what he was going to talk about and then he restated it half a dozen times throughout his reading of the text. And wouldn't you know it, he stated it again in his conclusion. His point, "God disciplines the disobedient." The text, 1 Kings 13, one of the strangest stories in the Bible. One of the most unforgettable messages I've ever heard.

What my professor lacked in style he more than made up for in clarity. He came to make one point and he made it. We had dozens of chapel speakers. Some of them quite famous. I couldn't tell you one thing they said. But the guy who was quite possibly the most unpopular man on campus made one unforgettable point. Moral of the story, *clarity trumps style*. Clarity trumps just about everything.

FACE IT

Don't defend bad communication habits with the line, "Well that's not my style." Let's be honest, for many communicators "style" means a combination of bad habits. Habits they don't even know they have. But habits that have shaped them as a communicator and have shaped their reputation. Don't hide behind style to excuse a lack of clarity. Please don't use style as an excuse not to engage your audience.

Think about it this way. What if I came to you and said, "If you will start doing the following four things when you speak, your audience size will double in a month. Not only that, your personal income will double as well." Would you try it? Or would you look at the list and say, "Gee, I don't know. I'm not really comfortable with that. That's not my style."

Obviously I can't (and wouldn't if I could) guarantee results from applying anything in this book. That's not my point. My point is that there is something out there that would motivate you to quit hiding behind the "that's not my style" excuse and work to become a better communicator. It may not be the size of your audience or money, but there's something that would move you to try some new things and take some new risks.

What if you had a sixteen-year-old son who said he was coming to church one last time and then he was packing up and hitting the road for good. And what if in the middle of the night an angel appeared and said, "You can reach the heart of your son if you do exactly what I tell you. Go into your attic and find his old box of Legos. On Sunday preach a message around this one point: *Christ came to build a bridge to the disconnected.* The entire time you are preaching you are to construct a bridge using his Legos." I know it's far-fetched. However, I also know that somebody reading this book is going to go find some Legos and build a bridge next Sunday.

If that really happened to you, I feel confident that you would not respond by saying, "But I'm not good with visual aids." Neither would you say, "I can't do that in my church, it would require removing the pulpit." If you really believed that getting way outside your comfort zone on a Sunday morning would reach your teenage son, you would do it. If you wouldn't, there are probably other books you should be reading.

Now please don't miss this. Next Sunday, somebody's prodigal son or daughter may slip into the back of your auditorium to give the God thing one last try. And it could very well be that somewhere in your town there is a mom or dad praying like crazy that something significant would happen in the heart of their child. I know you would be willing to do some new and possibly unusual things to reach your own son or daughter. What would you be willing to do to reach someone else's?

In the past four years we have experienced a big influx of adults in their late fifties and sixties. Do you know why they come? Because we have reached their young adult children. Our "style" is not necessarily their "style," but they are willing to make adjustments in order to be in church with their kids; kids they weren't sure would ever engage with a church. They have adjusted their style in order to worship with their kids. Shouldn't we be willing to adjust ours to reach their kids? Boring, confusing, complicated, scattered, and dry are all communication styles. But they are not styles worth defending. They are styles that should be abandoned.

GOAL AND STYLE

In chapter 11 I challenged you to identify your goal as a communicator and then choose an approach that supports your goal. Here I am challenging you to develop a style that supports your goal as well. If your goal is changed lives then you must develop a style that facilitates that goal. As you are probably aware, churches are notorious for having a mission statement hanging on the wall that is not supported by what's actually happening down the hall. Similarly, I've listened to dozens of preachers and teachers whose stated purpose for communicating is changed lives but whose style of communication doesn't support their purpose. If you are not willing to make adjustments for the sake of your goal then one thing is clear: Your goal is something other than changed lives. Your goal is to keep doing what you've always done, to do what's comfortable.

Think for a moment about some of the communicators who have captured the attention of the evangelical community in America over the past ten years: Rob Bell, Tony Evans, Louie Giglio, Bill Hybels, Beth Moore, Rick Warren, and Ed Young. They have things in common. But they come to the platform with their own unique style of communication. They are all engaging. But they are not all funny. Each drives the listener to a point of application. But they don't get there the same way. They are all committed to the Scriptures. But the way they approach the Scriptures varies. Some are intense while others are gregarious. Ed, Louie, and Rob make frequent use of visuals. The others do not. Bill is comfortable with a manuscript. Rick is comfortable with fill in the blank. Louie is comfortable with not knowing exactly what he is going to talk about until he arrives and sizes up an audience.

There is no one correct style. But there are principles that each of these individuals draw from. Each has a slightly different approach. But they all communicate for life change. Each has adopted a style that fits their personality. But they all connect with a variety of audiences.

TWO DECISIONS

In your quest to develop an effective style you need to constantly ask yourself two questions:

1. What works?
2. What works for me?

The first question will keep you on the lookout for new principles and methods of communication. It will drive you to wonder why certain communicators are so engaging and why others are not. It will keep you open to new ideas. It will motivate you to be a lifelong learner in the field of communication. Hopefully this book gave you some further insight into what works.

The second question will motivate you to continually evaluate and tweak your delivery. It will drive you to listen to and (if you are really a glutton for punishment) watch your own messages. Howard Hendricks says, "Experience doesn't make you better. Only evaluated experience makes you better." During seminary I taught a Sunday school class to seven college students. I taped every one and drove around on Sunday nights listening. I still listen to my own CDs. On some occasions I will listen to my message from all three services. I remember sitting with my dad as a kid as he watched his own videos.

Not too long ago I heard a man preach who paused between every five or six sentences. He would just stop talking. It was only a second or two. But it happened throughout his message. I knew what he was doing. He was thinking. It was extremely distracting. It communicated insecurity. And granted, we've all got some insecurities, but the last thing you want to do is advertise them every time you stand up to speak. As I listened I had two thoughts: I bet he's never seen a video of himself speaking. And secondly, this is something he could fix if he ever became aware of it.

You will never figure out what works and what doesn't listening to the casual comments of your constituents. And your spouse won't be much help either. If you want to improve, you are going to have to listen to yourself and ask for constructive criticism. Neither are any fun. I would much rather listen to your CD than mine.

Figure out what works. Figure out what works for you. This is the only way for you to become the gift to the world of teaching and preaching that God intended for you to be.

Find your voice.

TAKEAWAY

- Being yourself is not an excuse for poor communication habits.

- Be yourself. But become the best communicator *yourself* can be.

- Continually ask yourself, *What works? What works for me?*

17

START ALL OVER

What's the next step?

It's Saturday afternoon. I just double-clicked my Word document titled "Pause #1/forty-one Days." We are launching a new four-part series tomorrow morning. I've been working on it for a month. In fact, I've completed the first three messages. And I was feeling pretty good about all that until just a few minutes ago when I read through my outline for tomorrow. I haven't looked at it since I finished it three weeks ago. Actually, I just *thought* I finished it, because it is looking pretty rough right now. Way too long. Too many ideas. I picked a point. But it is not very moving. There is no *one thing* holding this thing together. Instead, there are many *things*. I've got some work to do. But honestly, I'm not sure where to begin.

Fortunately, I have a plan to help me get from where I am to where I need to be. That wasn't always the case. But a few years ago I discovered two things that help me get the traction I need to move beyond the confusion and complexity that frequently plagues my preparation. And after reading through this outline for the third time, it is safe to say I need some traction. This message doesn't really go anywhere.

Two hours and twenty minutes later and I'm feeling a lot better. I may not need to call in sick after all. In fact, I'm pretty excited about this one. That's always the case when I pick a point and build everything around it. But sometimes I get stuck. And stuck is a scary place to be for people in our business. Especially on Saturday night.

FACE DOWN

We all get stuck every once in a while. Honestly, I get stuck a lot. By stuck I mean that deep into my preparation I realize that I'm continuing to add information but it's not really taking me anywhere. I know I'm stuck when I have several pages of notes but no big idea. I know I'm stuck when nothing I have written or discovered moves me. I know I'm stuck when what I thought was a great idea suddenly goes in three or four unrelated directions.

For those of us who communicate weekly, getting stuck can be a terrifying thing. Sunday's coming whether we have anything significant to say or not. People are going to show up expecting to hear something they have never heard before. Some of 'em will even bring friends. So we can't afford to stay stuck long.

So what do you do when you are stuck?

The first thing I do when I get stuck is pray. But I'm not talking about a quick, *Help me Lord, Sunday's a comin' prayer.* When I get stuck I get up from my desk to head for my closet. Literally. If I'm at the office I go over to a corner that I have deemed my closet away from home. I get on my knees and remind God that this was not my idea, it was His. He let me volunteer. I confess that every opportunity I have to open His word in front of people comes from Him and that anything helpful I've ever said came from Him.

None of this is new information for God. I've been reminding Him for years.

Then I ask God to show me if there is something He wants to say to prepare me for what He wants me to communicate to our congregation. I surrender my ideas, my outline, and my topic. Then I just stay in that quiet place until God quiets my heart. It may be a few minutes. It may be much longer. There are times when absolutely nothing changes other than a decrease in my anxiety level. On some occasions something I need to deal with in my personal life will surface. That's always a lot of fun. Seems like bad timing. But God certainly has my undivided attention when the pressure's on. Many times while praying I will have a breakthrough thought or idea that brings clarity to my message.

I don't know why God chooses to work this way in my life. But I do know the outcome. I am constantly reminded that it is not my education, insights, or study habits that change lives. ME-WE-GOD-YOU-WE is helpful, but on its own it is not transformational. At the end of the day, it is God who empowers people to change. It is the Holy Spirit who opens the eyes of the heart. It is our Savior who gives men and women the courage to love and forgive. I, like you, am simply a mouthpiece. Getting stuck is one way God keeps me ever conscious of that fact.

If I don't stop and pray, the pressure to *get the message finished* will override my passion to bring something fresh and clear to my audience. When I ignore the impulse to pray, I find myself churning out information rather than creating an easy to follow journey for the listener. You may be thinking, *Gee, don't you pray before you study? Is praying a last resort?* No. I pray before, during, and after! I'm just telling you what I do when I get stuck.

THE LIST

On those occasions when I emerge from my closet with peace but no new thoughts I move to the second phase of my strategy for getting unstuck. I call one of our other staff communicators and ask them to preach.

Not really.

If I still lack clarity I go back to basics. I pull out my trusted list of questions and start over. By start over I don't mean I trash everything I've done up until that point. But instead of trying to bring order to the ocean of words on my computer screen I focus my attention on answering five questions. These questions enable me to sort through the many ideas and help me land on the one around which I need to organize my message. When I have a succinct answer to these five questions, organizing my material is a cinch.

1. What do they need to know?

We talked about this in chapter 12. As committed as I am to organizing messages around one central idea, it is still easy for me to drift during my preparation. So I have to stop, push back from my desk, and think, *in light of what I've discovered from the text and the insights I've gained along the way, what is the one thing they need to know?* This is the point at which I sometimes get up and take a lap around the parking lot.

Forcing yourself to answer this question will probably mean that much of what is staring at you from your computer screen will not make it into your message. This too can be terrifying. Possibly discouraging. You may feel like you have wasted a lot of time. But you haven't. There's always next week. Besides, finding the one thing usually requires digging through a dozen other things. That's just part of the process. The real issue is whether you have the discipline to stick with your point and not try to force *everything* into your message.

Then of course there is the fear of, *How am I going to fill the time?* Fear not, we've only covered the first question. And if you are like most communicators, filling your time is probably not a relevant concern. If you would worry less about filling up the time and focus your attention on building your message around one clear and compelling idea you will win on both fronts. You will fill your time, but better yet, you will keep your audience engaged throughout the time.

Be honest. What is the one thing that needs to be communicated?

2. Why do they need to know it?

Here's a question very few communicators take time to answer for their audience. And that's too bad. Because when you answer this question you give your listeners a reason to keep listening. If you fail to answer this one, you are assuming a level of interest that may not be there.

In many Christian circles the assumption is, if the Bible says it, that's enough. We don't need a *why* just a *what.* And that works for a percentage of Christians. But it doesn't work for the other half and it doesn't work at all for people who don't view the Bible as authoritative.

Let me rephrase the question:

- What will happen to the person who never discovers the truth or principle you are about to address?
- What is at stake for them?

When I unearth the *why* behind the *what* I begin to feel passionate about my subject. When I have an answer for this question I realize just how important my message really is. This is where the burden comes from. After all, there is a lot at stake.

Think about the last talk you gave. Why was that message important? Why should anyone have taken you seriously? Why did your audience need to know what you told them? At any point in your message did you tell them why what you had to say was important?

In just about every message I give I will say, "Here's why this is important…." Often I will break it down. "If you are a teenager, here's why you need to listen closely this morning. If you are married this principle has huge implications for your marriage. If you are in a difficult relationship, I'm really glad you are here for this. This truth could make all the difference."

I usually explain *why* at the end of the introduction. Now that they know *where* we are going, they need to know *why* I'm taking 'em there. The fact that it is in the Bible is enough for some, but not enough for most. Answering *why* provides an incentive for your audience to follow you to the next part of your message. If listeners are not convinced they need to know what you are about to tell them, they will consider your information irrelevant.

Once I have discovered *why* they need to know what I'm about to tell them, I move on to the third question.

3. What do they need to do?

This doesn't come as a surprise. And the question certainly isn't original with me. But I'm shocked at how few communicators really take this question to heart. Every message you deliver has at least one point of application. Discover what it is and then state it.

What do you want them to do in response to what you've said?

My two recommendations on this point are: Be specific and be creative. Give your audience something very specific to do. Something so specific they will know immediately whether or not they have done it. If it is a lifestyle issue, make a suggestion as to how long they should do it.

For example, if the focus of your message is on the importance of personal prayer, it is not enough to end by saying, "So pray!" That may be what you want them to do, but that's not specific enough. At the same time I would not suggest that you stand up and ask people in your audience to make a commitment to pray every day for the rest of their lives. That's specific but unrealistic.

When I ask an audience to do something specific, I usually ask them to commit to a specific length of time. Halfway through a series on the Lord's prayer I asked our congregation to begin the next seven days with prayer. Just seven days. Anybody could do that. And hopefully those seven days would begin a habit.

In addition to being specific, be creative. For example, when I challenged our congregation to begin keeping track of their expenses I gave them a ledger sheet and asked them to keep track for one month. Giving them a ledger sheet was creative. Giving them a time frame was specific. They would know immediately if they had done what I had asked them to do. Sometimes a single application can run the length of a series. That way you have several weeks to instill the value of what you suggested they do.

Once you have narrowed the application to something specific it is time to answer the fourth question.

4. Why do they need to do it?

The first time you answered *why* you inspired them to keep listening. Now you've got to inspire them to action. Why should they do what you have suggested?

"It should be obvious," you object. And you are right. It should be. But go ahead and spend a few minutes thinking through exactly what's at stake if they don't follow through. Make a list. And then put it in your outline. Then tell 'em. After you explain *what*, tell them *why*. Answering *why* at this juncture serves as the perfect segue into the WE section of your message.

> "Imagine what would happen if all of us went to work tomorrow with renewed commitment to serve those who usually serve us."

"Imagine what would happen in our families if every one of us made a list of the relational debts we felt that others owed us and then cancelled those debts."

"Imagine how much joy we could generate as a congregation if every one of us sat down this week and wrote a thank-you letter to the person who introduced us to Christ."

Once I answer those four questions I'm not only unstuck, I'm excited. The first two get me to the text. The last two get me to the finish line. But there is one additional question I always ask. This isn't really part of my unstuck strategy, but it is part of my preparation. So here it is. The fifth and final question.

5. What can I do to help them remember?

What can I do to help them remember either my point or my application? The ledger sheet I referenced earlier was an answer to that question. We almost always hand out memory verse cards to go with our series. When I finished my series on Jonah, I gave everybody a flower and asked them to associate that with whatever it was in their lives that was more important to them than people's souls. Then I asked them to put it somewhere where they could watch it slowly die. It was a way of remembering.

We've given away refrigerator magnets, doughnuts, pieces of canvas, paint brushes, compasses, stickers, CDs, books, bottles of beads, water bottles, and money. We don't do that every week. Again, I don't always have a good answer to this question. But I always ask it. And every once in a while something surfaces that makes a big impact.

Here they are again:

1. What do they need to know?   INFORMATION
2. Why do they need to know it?   MOTIVATION
3. What do they need to do?   APPLICATION
4. Why do they need to do it?   INSPIRATION
5. How can I help them remember?   REITERATION

Here's my suggestion. Make a copy of these questions and keep them where you study. When you get stuck, start at the top. When you are finished, check and see if you have answered the first four. If you have, pull together a team and chew on that last one.

Everybody gets stuck. Sometimes it has nothing to do with our ability to organize content. That's why we need to stop and pray. Sometimes we just get lost in the information. That's why we need some questions to get us going and keep us going until we have discovered the one thing that the people God has entrusted to our care need to know.

TAKEAWAY

- Don't allow the pressure to *get the sermon finished* override your passion to bring something fresh to your audience.

- When you get stuck, pray!

- When you get stuck, go back to basics: What do they need to know? Why do they need to know it? What do they need to do? Why do they need to do it? How can I help them remember?

CONCLUSION

Writing a book about communication is a bit like writing a book about playing the piano. It has its limits. We sure hope you found something here that you can begin applying immediately. And perhaps in the near future you will try your hand at developing and communicating a one point message. With this approach, multiple points will give way to mileposts that mark your progress towards a single destination. Introductions will create the tension you want to resolve or raise the question you intend to answer. Application will be the driving force of the message, rather than a section tacked on to the end. In my experience, this is a much easier and more effective way to approach communicating the Scriptures.

The church needs your voice and your insight. As does your community and the world. For that reason, never stop growing and developing as a communicator. Find what works. Find what works for you. And every time you have an opportunity to communicate God's Word, communicate for a change!

How long do you preach?

Forty minutes.

How long is a typical series?

Four to six weeks.

Are you involved in the creative planning for the service?

Yes. Very. I attend two meetings each week to plan and evaluate the weekend services. In addition I have quarterly meetings we refer to as "content meetings." This is where I gather random staff to brainstorm through a topic. Then Julie Arnold, our service program division director, leads a creative team meeting to flesh out the creative theme for a series.

How far out do you plan?

We plan conceptually for an entire year. We plan a specific series three months out. We do not give all our series equal support. We do three big series each year. Between those we will do more scaled-down series.

Do you ever repeat a message?

I will often repackage a message from a series and use it in a different series. We've never repeated an entire series as it was originally presented.

ME-WE-GOD-YOU-WE

1. What do they need to know?   INFORMATION

2. Why do they need to know it?   MOTIVATION

3. What do they need to do?   APPLICATION

4. Why do they need to do it?   INSPIRATION

5. How can I help them remember?   REITERATION